Preschool 1 Bulletin Boards

by
Linda J. Liljehorn

illustrated by
Elizabeth Nygaard

Cover by Jeff Van Kanegan

Shining Star Publications, Copyright © 1991
A Division of Good Apple

ISBN No. 0-86653-572-1

Standardized Subject Code TA ac

Printing No. 987654321

Shining Star Publication
A Division of Good Apple
1204 Buchanan St., Box 299
Carthage, IL 62321-0299

Unless otherwise indicated, the King James Version of the Bible was used in preparing the activities in this book.

Simon & Schuster Supplementary Education Group

DEDICATION

Dedicated to the staff of the Trinity Child Care Center in Holdrege, Nebraska. Many thanks for giving me opportunities throughout the years to S-T-R-E-T-C-H my creativity. This book's for you!

With special love and appreciation to my family, Roger, Tiffany, Mark and Michael. Thanks for all of your support and for loving me in spite of myself.

SS896

TO THE TEACHER

Is it time to decorate your bulletin boards again? Do you want to provide more than just a colorful display in order to help your students learn some of God's lessons?

If you answered yes to these questions, *Preschool Bible Bulletin Boards* is for you. Within these pages you will discover bulletin board designs, crafts and circle time activities. The circle time activities include discussion questions for older children, songs to familiar tunes, recitations, finger plays and stories.

The easiest way to transfer the bulletin board ideas from this book to your bulletin boards is to use an overhead projector. Simply trace the design on a transparency and project it onto the wall. You may trace the pattern from this allowing you to make the design whatever size you wish simply by moving the projector.

You will find a few patterns in the back of the book. Some of them will be needed for crafts while others may be used for borders or name tags or to be hung from the ceiling. Be flexible; use your imagination.

Hopefully these ideas will help you plan holiday and seasonal activities that will be fun as well as educational.

Blessings to you!

TABLE OF CONTENTS

MAKE A JOYFUL NOISE

scissors

tape

oatmeal

markers

paper to put around drum

What's a happy sound? A JOYFUL NOISE! This display is a celebration of our joy in Jesus. Use bright, contrasting colors for the best effect. The tassel on the party hat can be made of tissue paper, yarn, etc. For a three-dimensional effect, use scissors to curl ribbon and staple or glue it to the board. Colored scraps of paper can be glued to the board to represent confetti. If desired, a border of party hats and horns can be added. For an additional decoration, party hats can be hung from the ceiling. (See pattern on page 95.)

Shining Star Publications, Copyright © 1991, A division of Good Apple   SS896

MAKE A JOYFUL NOISE

PURPOSE: A just-for-fun board that focuses on what kinds of noises are fun and acceptable and what kinds are not.

SUGGESTED BIBLE VERSE: "Make a joyful noise unto the Lord. . . ." Psalm 98:4a

TABLE ACTIVITY: Make oatmeal box drums.

MATERIALS: Oatmeal boxes, white paper, markers, tape.

PROCEDURE: Prior to class, cut the oatmeal boxes in half. Measure and mark paper the correct width to fit the boxes. Older children should be able to cut along the line on the paper. The teacher may need to cut the paper for younger children. All children will enjoy decorating the paper. When finished, tape paper to the box. Now you have a drum. Make a joyful noise!

DISCUSSION: What kinds of noises do you think are okay? What kinds of noises do you think are not okay? Have you ever heard someone in church sing off-key? Maybe you laughed. Did you know God was pleased with the person who was singing if that person was singing with a joyful heart? Do you think the Lord is pleased with the noise we make when we laugh and make fun of someone? What are some ways you can make a joyful noise?

CIRCLE TIME ACTIVITIES

Recitation

It makes me happy when I sing,
All praises to my God and King!

To the tune of "Fishers of Men"

I can sing my praise unto Him,
Praise unto Him, praise unto Him;
I can sing my praise unto Him
I can SHOUT and sing.
I can SHOUT and sing,
I can SHOUT and sing;
I can sing my praise unto Him,
I can SHOUT and sing.

An Action Recitation

How does the Lord feel when I laugh,
(act like laughing)
At those who are diff'rent from me,
(point to self)
It doesn't make Him very glad,
(shake head sideways)
And it hurts them, too, you see.
(nod)

Recitation

I can make a happy sound,
Because I know I'm heaven bound!

HE LEADETH ME

HE LEADETH ME is the caption for this display showing the hand of God leading a little child. A piece of white material can be draped and used for Jesus' robe. Artificial flowers will also help add a special effect. A border of footprints may be added to tie the board's theme and the table activity together. Footprints may also be placed on the walls in the classroom. They may go up, down and all around. (See pattern on page 95.)

 SS896

HE LEADETH ME

PURPOSE: To impress upon students that the Lord leads our lives when we fully trust in Him.

SUGGESTED BIBLE VERSE: "Lead me in thy truth, and teach me . . . on thee do I wait all the day." Psalm 25:5

TABLE ACTIVITY: Make individual footprints.

MATERIALS: White construction paper, paint, black marker.

PROCEDURE: Trace around child's foot. The child may paint his footprint. As a final step, the teacher may write *He Leadeth* _____ (child's name) along side of the footprint.

DISCUSSION: Who leads our lives? I'm going to read Psalm 48:14. Listen closely please. According to our verse, how long is God our God? How long does He guide us? Also read Psalm 73:24 to the children.

CIRCLE TIME ACTIVITIES

Recitation

A new year's here.
What can I say?
My God leads me day by day.

To the tune of "Deep and Wide"

He leads me.
He leads me.
He leads me everywhere I go.
He leads me.
He leads me.
He leads me everywhere I go.

Recitation

My God shows me what to do;
I know that He will help you, too.

Finger Play

My God walks beside me
(make fingers walk)
Everywhere I go.
That is why I'm happy;
(smile)
He cares for me, I know.
(nod)

An Action Recitation

Step, step, step,
I will walk with God;
Step, step, step,
I will walk with God.

SS896

A BUNCH O' LOVE

A BUNCH O' LOVE is a colorful display that focuses on slightly heart-shaped balloons. Use brightly colored paper for balloons with contrasting ribbon or yarn for strings. The children's table activity will follow the same balloon pattern and may be bunched together and fastened at each corner of the display.

A BUNCH O' LOVE

PURPOSE: A fun way to talk about God loving us so much, He saved us.

SUGGESTED BIBLE VERSE: "Greater love hath no man than this, that a man lay down his life for his friends." John 15:13

TABLE ACTIVITY: Make heart-shaped paper balloons.

MATERIALS: Pattern on page 95, oaktag, brightly colored construction paper, white paper, glue, scissors, black marker, markers, ribbon or yarn.

PROCEDURE: Prior to class, make a balloon pattern the size of a sheet of paper. Due to the message, the balloons should be a modified heart shape. To achieve this, fold a paper as you would to cut out a heart. When you get to the place where the bottom point would be formed, cut straight to the end. (For younger children, the teacher will need to cut out the balloon shape; for older ones, they may cut them out themselves.) All children can decorate their balloons with markers or crayons. Have each child glue a ribbon or yarn to the bottom of their balloon. The teacher or another adult may write *God Is Love* on the balloon with a black marker.

DISCUSSION: Does God love us? How does he show us His love? He shows us He loves us by giving us food, clothing, a home and a family. There's something very special He did for us that will affect us forever and ever. Can you tell me what it is? Our Bible verse for today talks about it. Isn't it exciting to know we have a friend like God?

CIRCLE TIME ACTIVITIES

To the tune of "Frere Jacques"

God loves me.
God loves me.
He's my friend.
He's my friend.
God loves me each morning.
God loves me each morning.
He's my friend, to the end.

To the tune of "The Farmer in the Dell"

God loves me all the time.
God loves me all the time.
Hi, ho, He loves me so;
God loves me all the time.

Recitation

I am happy as can be,
Our God really does love me!

LOVE BEARS ALL THINGS

It is hard to be perfect like Jesus. Sometimes our feelings get hurt. LOVE BEARS ALL THINGS is a display which demonstrates some of the burdens kids bear today. Try to find pictures that illustrate the emotions described in each heart. Cut out the pictures in the shape of hearts. Trim with pinking shears for a decorative effect. Feel free to add pictures of other burdens you may find appropriate. (See pattern on page 95.)

LOVE BEARS ALL THINGS

PURPOSE: To talk about how the Lord can help us deal with the problems that come into our lives.

SUGGESTED BIBLE VERSE: ". . . forbearing one another in love." Ephesians 4:2b

TABLE ACTIVITY: Make a heart necklace.

MATERIALS: Salt dough (3 cups of flour, ¾ cup of salt, 1¼-1½ cups cold water), heart-shaped cookie cutters, cookie sheet, slips of paper or oaktag with Ephesians 4:2b on them, paper punch, yarn, paint and paint brushes.

PROCEDURE: Prior to class, prepare dough. If your class consists of smaller children, you will need to roll out the dough. Using cookie cutters, let the children cut out a heart or hearts to make their necklaces. Place on cookie sheet. Poke a hole in the top of each heart. Bake in 250 degree oven for 2 hours. Shut off oven and leave hearts in until oven has cooled. Paint. (Do not use powdered tempera or watercolors because they tend to be too wet.) Punch a hole in the Bible verse. String heart(s) and Bible verse onto a piece of yarn and tie.

DISCUSSION: Has anyone ever hurt your feelings? How did it make you feel? Boys and girls, I'm going to read some Bible verses. Can you listen carefully and see if you can tell me how the Bible says we are to treat those who have hurt us? (Find the answer in the following verses: I Peter 3:8,9; James 1:19,20.)

CIRCLE TIME ACTIVITIES

To the tune of "Oh Be Careful"

I get mad at you when you laugh at me.
I get mad at you when you laugh at me.
When you laugh it hurts me so,
I just wish you'd turn and go.
I get mad at you when you laugh at me.

A Story

Sometimes we get our feelings hurt. We can feel sad, angry or a little bit of both. Here is a story.

Bobby was new in town. It was scary to not know anyone. Bobby's mom and dad said the best way to meet people is to find a church to go to. And that's just what they did.

The first Sunday they went to church Bobby also went to Sunday school. His family always went to Sunday school before they moved. Most of the kids were very nice, but a little boy named Jamey said, "Hey, Bobby, your ears look like they belong to an elephant. We'll call you Ella, short for elephant."

Bobby began to turn red. He wanted to cry. He knew his ears were big. Why did Jamey have to ruin his first day in Sunday school? Poor Bobby. What would you have done if you were Bobby?

SS896

GOD OF OUR FATHERS

GOD OF OUR FATHERS is a display that can be used for President's month. The Bible between the two silhouettes indicates the faith of our forefathers. It was this faith that helped make our country great. A border of red, white and blue streamers will make an attractive board. You may also want to consider hanging red, white and blue stars from your ceiling.

SS896

GOD OF OUR FATHERS

PURPOSE: To point out that our Presidents depend on God to help them make big decisions that affect our nation.

SUGGESTED BIBLE VERSE: "Be still, and know that I am God." Psalm 46:10a NIV

TABLE ACTIVITY: Make no-bake cookies! M-m-m.

MATERIALS: 1¾ cup sugar, ⅔ cup milk, 2 teaspoons vanilla, 6 tablespoons peanut butter, ¼ pound soda crackers (crumbled).

PROCEDURE: Mix sugar and milk in a saucepan. Boil 3 minutes. Remove from heat. Add peanut butter, crumbled crackers and vanilla. Stir well. Spray a 9" x 9" pan with non-stick coating, and put mixture in the pan. Pat down, let cool and cut.

DISCUSSION: What is a President? Do you know who our President is? Two very important Presidents were George Washington and Abraham Lincoln. Both Washington and Lincoln tried to do what was right and to learn. The best thing about them was that they loved God. God gave them strength to help make our country great. Many Presidents have said that without God's help, they wouldn't know how to lead our country. Abraham Lincoln's picture is on our penny; George Washington's picture is on our dollar bill. The words say, "In God We Trust." Isn't it nice to know that someone as important as a President loves and depends on God, too? Can you think of other Presidents who loved and depended on God?

CIRCLE TIME ACTIVITIES

To the tune of "Deep and Wide"

Presidents, Presidents,
They lead our country, Presidents;
Presidents, Presidents,
They lead our country, Presidents.

To the tune of "Fishers of Men"

Presidents need our God to lead,
Our God to lead,
Our God to lead;
Presidents need our God to lead
When they make a choice.
When they make a choice,
When they make a choice;
Presidents need our God to lead
When they make a choice.

To the tune of "The B-I-B-L-E"

A President is great,
When he is never late,
To pray each day to our God above,
A President is great.

Recitation

Presidents are really great,
When on God's word they meditate.

SS896

PRAYER CHANGES THINGS

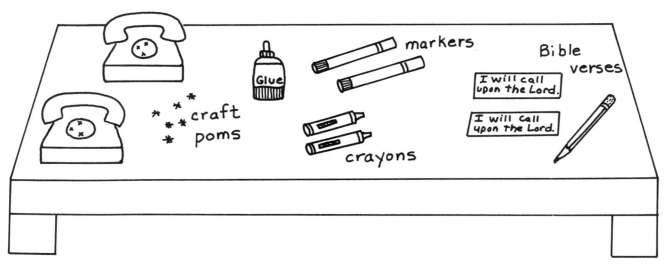

What can a child do when he's scared, lonely or sad? He can pray, because PRAYER CHANGES THINGS. This board may be used anytime a day of prayer is designated. The craft is used to complete the board. Brightly colored clothing on the child helps add interest. (See border pattern on page 96.)

      SS896

PRAYER CHANGES THINGS

PURPOSE: To stress to students the importance of prayer. To instill in them the knowledge that God sees and answers prayer.

SUGGESTED BIBLE VERSE: "I will call upon the Lord. . . ." Psalm 18:3a

TABLE ACTIVITY: Create paper telephones for the bulletin board.

MATERIALS: Oaktag, telephone pattern on page 79, small craft pom-poms, glue, slips of paper, crayons or markers.

PROCEDURE: Prior to class, trace and cut out telephone. Write Psalm 18:3a on slips of paper. Have the children color their phones. Mark an *X* where each number on a phone would be located. Allow children to glue pom-poms onto each *X.* When the children are finished with their activity, attach the Bible verse to each phone.

DISCUSSION: What is prayer? Prayer is when we talk to God. Do we call Him on a telephone? That's silly. Of course we don't call Him on the phone. But it's just as easy as that to pray. We can pray to God when we're happy, sad, lonely or scared. We can pray to God at any time, day or night. God hears us when we pray. We know He does because the Bible says so in I John 5:14b. Listen carefully as I read from the Bible. Should we only pray for the things we want or need? No. The Bible tells us in James 5:16b to pray for one another. ("Pray one for another.") I'm glad I can call upon the Lord, aren't you?

CIRCLE TIME ACTIVITIES

To the tune of "Row, Row, Row Your Boat"

I can pray each day to my God on high;
I can pray and pray and pray
To my God on high.

To the tune of "Skip to My Lou"

I will pray to my precious Lord.
I will pray to my precious Lord.
I will pray to my precious Lord.
I will pray and pray.
Pray, pray, yes, I will pray.
Pray, pray, yes, I will pray.
Pray, pray, yes, I will pray.
I will pray to Jesus.

Recitation

Thank you, Lord, for hearing me,
When in prayer I call on Thee.

To the tune of "Oh Be Careful"

I can call on God in prayer everyday.
I can call on God in prayer everyday.
I can call on God in prayer
And I know He's always there.
I can call on God in prayer everyday.

SS896

GOD'S LOVE SETS US FREE

GOD'S LOVE SETS US FREE is the caption for this display featuring butterflies. It may be pointed out to the children that when Jesus sets us free from sin, it makes us happy. Bright colors make this display one to which children will be drawn. (See border pattern on page 96.)

   SS896

GOD'S LOVE SETS US FREE

PURPOSE: To encourage children to visualize the difference Christ can make, using a cocoon and butterfly as an object lesson.

SUGGESTED BIBLE VERSE: "Stand fast therefore in the liberty by which Christ has made us free." Galatians 5:1a NKJV

TABLE ACTIVITY: Make butterfly mosaics.

MATERIALS: Various colors of poster board, shell macaroni, glitter, butterfly pattern from page 79, scissors.

PROCEDURE: Prior to class, make a pattern of the butterfly. Trace around and cut out butterflies. During class children can glue on macaroni. As a final step, brush the macaroni with glue and sprinkle with glitter.

DISCUSSION: How many of you have seen a cocoon? Was it pretty? What was in the cocoon? What happens to the cocoon after the caterpillar has been in it awhile? It breaks open. That is what it is like for a person who doesn't know Jesus; his life is ugly because of sin. But slowly he begins to struggle. He begins asking himself what's right and wrong. Finally, he asks the Lord into his heart. He breaks away from the ugliness of sin. Because of Jesus, he is free.

CIRCLE TIME ACTIVITIES
The Wonderful Change
(A Pantomime with Narration)

Once upon a time, there was an ugly little fellow whose name was Waldo Worm. Many of the other animals and insects in the garden would make fun of Waldo because he was so plain. "You're ugly," they would say. Sadly, Waldo grew to believe that he was indeed ugly.

One day, Waldo felt the strangest thing. He felt like something or someone was telling him to climb up on a branch. It wasn't that crawling on a branch was unusual, it was just the funny feeling he had. Slowly, Waldo crawled to a tree. Then he pulled himself up the tree and onto a branch. The strange feeling continued and soon he found himself spinning a funny little house. When he was done he was so tired he decided to take a nap.

Now, when Waldo awakened, he didn't know how long he had been asleep. It was hard for him to move. Why is it so hard to move? he thought. All Waldo knew was that he had to get out of wherever he was. Slowly he struggled. Little by little he felt his house breaking. Finally he was free. When he tried to crawl, he couldn't—but he could fly!

When his friends came he said, "Look, I'm beautiful!" "You are BEAUTIFUL!" all of his friends agreed. The ugliness was gone. Waldo was so happy! He thanked the Lord, for it was God who had helped him to take his long nap. It was because of God that he was free.

To the tune of "This Old Man"
I am free, I am free;
'Cause of Jesus I am free.
I am free and happy as can be;
'Cause of Jesus I am free.

Recitation
I can live eternally,
All because He set me free.

Shining Star Publications, Copyright © 1991, A division of Good Apple

SS896

THERE SHALL BE SHOWERS OF BLESSINGS

SHOWERS OF BLESSINGS is what the Lord sends to His children. This board is designed to help children focus on the good things God gives them. The umbrella should be a bright color. The raindrops on the display may be covered with plastic wrap for a wet look. (See umbrella pattern on page 96.)

SS896

THERE SHALL BE SHOWERS OF BLESSINGS

PURPOSE: To draw attention to blessings children can enjoy.

SUGGESTED BIBLE VERSE: "Blessings are upon the head of the just." Proverbs 10:6a

TABLE ACTIVITY: Make "wet" raindrops.

MATERIALS: Raindrop pattern on page 80, white paper, blue paint, plastic wrap, slips of paper, markers, tape, scissors.

PROCEDURE: Older children may cut out their raindrops. For younger children, it will be necessary for the teacher to cut them out. All children may paint their raindrops. Ask each child to name a blessing he enjoys. Write it on a slip of paper and have him glue it to his raindrop. When dry, cover with plastic wrap and secure.

DISCUSSION: What do you think the word *blessing* means? Where do you think blessings come from? Can you name some blessings you have received?

CIRCLE TIME ACTIVITIES

To the tune of "Here We Go 'Round the Mulberry Bush"

All blessings come from God above,
God above, God above.
All blessings come from God above;
I will thank Him now.

Program Recitation for Six Children

ALL: The Lord gives many blessings. Thank you, Lord.
#1: For our mommies,
ALL: We thank you, Lord!
#2: For our daddies,
ALL: We thank you, Lord!
#3: For our homes,
ALL: We thank you, Lord!
#4: For our friends,
ALL: We thank you, Lord!
#5: For all of us,
ALL: We thank you, Lord!
#6: For dying on the cross for us,
ALL: WE THANK YOU, LORD!

To the tune of "B-I-N-G-O"

I thank you, Lord, for all the things
That you have given me-e.
Thank you, oh my Lord.
Thank you, oh my Lord.
Thank you, oh my Lord
For all You've given me.

SS896

HE CARES FOR YOU

Sometimes children feel that they aren't very important. HE CARES FOR YOU is a display which features a giant birdhouse. It is important for children to realize that if God cares for the birds, He certainly cares for the children. In order for the children to contribute to the creation of the display, place their completed crafts on the bulletin board around the big birdhouse.

SS896

HE CARES FOR YOU

PURPOSE: To impress upon children that if God cares for the birds, how much more He cares for them!

SUGGESTED BIBLE VERSE: "Behold the fowls of the air. . .your heavenly Father feedeth them. Are ye not much better than they?" Matthew 6:26

TABLE ACTIVITY: Make a birdhouse.

MATERIALS: White construction paper, paint, paint brushes, glue, pattern for birdhouse and bird from page 81, typing paper.

PROCEDURE: Prior to class, trace and cut out birdhouses and birds on construction paper. Also, write on slips of typing paper the following Bible words: *He careth for you.* Children are to paint the birdhouses and birds. Have each child glue his bird to his birdhouse. When dry, glue the slips with the Bible words to each birdhouse. Arrange on the board to complete the display.

DISCUSSION: According to our Bibles, are birds important to God? Are we more or less important to God? Our Bibles tell us that we are much more important to Him than the birds. Isn't that exciting? Our Bible tells us we're special, so we know it's true.

CIRCLE TIME ACTIVITIES

To the tune of "Jesus Loves the Little Children of the World"

Our God feeds the little birdies,
All the birdies of the air;
One by one they all are fed,
To the food they're always led.
Our God feeds the little birdies of the air.

To the tune of "Fishers of Men"

God helps birds to eat and to live,
Eat and to live,
Eat and to live.
God helps birds to eat and to live;
Our God loves the birds.
Our God loves the birds;
Our God loves the birds.
God helps birds to eat and to live;
Our God loves the birds.

Finger Play

The birds up in the tree tops,
(throw arms in the air and wiggle fingers)
Are special as can be;
Our God feeds the little birds,
(act like scattering food)
And He feeds you and me!
(act like eating)

Recitation

Thank you, Lord, for loving me,
More than all the birds I see.

SS896

When we SING UNTO THE LORD A NEW SONG, it makes us happy. A happy time of year is spring. This display features a large, blue bird singing a happy springtime song. If you desire, black notes can be used as a border as well as hung from the ceiling. (See patterns on page 80.)

SING UNTO THE LORD A NEW SONG

PURPOSE: To stress that so often we say, "Lord, give me." A new song could be, "Thank you, Lord."

SUGGESTED BIBLE VERSE: "O Lord, open thou my lips: and my mouth shall show forth thy praise." Psalm 51:15

TABLE ACTIVITY: Make sculptured birds.

MATERIALS: Salt dough from page 12.

PROCEDURE: Have each child make a bird out of salt dough. When everyone is done, have a show-and-tell time when everyone can share their project and tell about a song they like to sing to the Lord.

DISCUSSION: What are some ways we can sing a new song? I'm going to read some verses. Listen carefully and maybe you can find the answer. (Read Psalm 106:1 and Psalm 107:1.)

CIRCLE TIME ACTIVITIES

To the tune of "He's Got the Whole World in His Hands"

The spring has come here once again.
The spring has come to earth once again.
The spring has come to earth once again;
I thank the Lord for spring today.

To the tune of "Twinkle, Twinkle, Little Star"

Our God made the trees of spring;
They are tall and lovely things.
I love spring, it brings me cheer;
It's my favorite time of year.
Our God made the trees of spring;
They are tall and lovely things.

To the tune of "London Bridge"

Happy spring comes once a year,
Once a year, once a year;
Happy spring comes once a year.
Thank you, Lord, for springtime.

Recitation

Spring brings sun and spring brings fun;
Spring comes when the winter's done.

To the tune of "Here We Go 'Round the Mulberry Bush"

Springtime comes and brings us fun,
Brings us fun,
Brings us fun.
Springtime comes and brings us fun;
Thank you, Lord, for springtime.

Recitation

S-P-R-I-N-G
Spring is a fun time for me.

  SS896

HOSANNA TO THE KING!

HOSANNA TO THE KING! What a happy sound. This display is a simple design that will add color to your classroom. The background can be a light gray or blue. Use a bright green for palm branches. If you want, fringe the edges of the palms. The crowns could be made of gold wrapping paper. Old earrings, necklace beads or buttons may be used for jewels. A double set of lettering may be made, one set of black and one of yellow. Use the black letters for the shadow and the yellow letters in the forefront. (See border pattern on page 96.)

SS896

HOSANNA TO THE KING!

PURPOSE: To show the way people demonstrated adoration for Jesus. To encourage the same response in children today.

SUGGESTED BIBLE VERSE: "Took branches of palm trees, and went forth to meet him, and cried, 'Hosanna.'" John 12:13a

TABLE ACTIVITY: Make palm branches.

MATERIALS: Palm branch pattern from page 82, dowel sticks (allow 6" for each child), tape, scissors.

PROCEDURE: Trace palm leaves. Older children may be able to cut out the leaf. Show children how to use scissors to "fringe" their leaves (short snips along outer edge). Tape dowel sticks to the back of leaf. HOSANNA!

DISCUSSION: Why do you think the people shouted "Hosanna" when Jesus came into Jerusalem? The word *Hosanna* was used in Bible times as a shout of welcome and as a shout of joy. The people were happy to see Jesus and so they welcomed Him by shouting "Hosanna."

CIRCLE TIME ACTIVITIES

To the tune of "The B-I-B-L-E"

(Use the palm branches the children made.)

Hosanna to the King,
Hosanna to the King,
We shout our praise to the Lord this day,
Hosanna to the King.

To the tune of "She'll Be Comin' 'Round the Mountain"

All the people sang "Hosanna" when He came.
All the people sang "Hosanna" when He came.
All the people sang "Hosanna,"
All the people sang "Hosanna,"
All the people sang "Hosanna" when He came.

To the tune of "Row, Row, Row Your Boat"

Ho-ho-Hosanna
All the people sang;
Ho-ho-ho-ho-ho-ho-ho
Hosanna they all sang.

To the tune of "Here We Go 'Round the Mulberry Bush"

Hosanna all the children sang,
The children sang,
The children sang;
Hosanna all the children sang,
Waving all their branches.

SS896

On Easter, one message stands out strong and clear: Christ arose! HE AROSE! is a very simple board that displays the central theme of the season. For the most effective color combination, use a light-blue background. Lay yellow and orange chalk sideways and make broad streaks on the light-blue paper. Put a few wisps of cotton on the background. Using royal blue construction paper, make *large* letters. Attach to board.

SS896

HE AROSE!

PURPOSE: To tell the children of Christ's resurrection.

SUGGESTED BIBLE VERSE: "And go quickly, and tell his disciples that he is risen from the dead." Matthew 28:7a

TABLE ACTIVITY: Make an empty tomb.

MATERIALS: Pattern on page 83, gray construction paper, brads, crayons or markers.

PROCEDURE: Prior to class reproduce enough sheets for everyone. Make a circle pattern big enough to cover the door of the tomb out of gray construction paper. If class members are younger, cut out the circles. Encourage children to color the pictures. Help them fasten the rock to the doorway using a brad placed on the X. Use the craft during circle time for the song "He's Not Here." (Roll away the stone with the first line of the song.)

DISCUSSION: Has anyone here had a grandparent who has died? How did it make you feel? I'm sure you missed him or her. The disciples missed Jesus. That is why they were so happy when he wasn't in the grave anymore. HE WAS ALIVE! Because Jesus died and rose, we can live with Him forever.

CIRCLE TIME ACTIVITIES

To the tune of "The Farmer in the Dell"

He rose for you and me,
He rose for you and me;
For our sins he bled and died,
And rose again you see.

To the tune of "Oh, Susanna"

Jesus died for you and died for me,
He loves us very much;
He arose again up from the grave,
He loves us very much.
Oh, He loves us; He loves us very much.
He arose again up from the grave;
He loves us very much.

Recitation

Jesus rose up from the grave,
So that He my soul could save.

To the tune of "Jesus Loves Me"

He's not here the angels said,
He has risen from the dead;
They can't keep Him in the grave,
He died so we could be saved.
Yes, He's not here.
Yes, He's not here.
Yes, He's not here;
He's risen from the dead.

SS896

A MOTHER'S LOVE COMES FROM GOD

paper

paint

brush

It is always nice to see a mother and child in a rocking chair. A MOTHER'S LOVE COMES FROM GOD is a display that demonstrates that love. Use soft pastels for Mom, a bright color for the child. A heart-shaped border would be appropriate.

SS896

A MOTHER'S LOVE COMES FROM GOD

PURPOSE: To let kids know moms need the Lord's help to be good mothers.

SUGGESTED BIBLE VERSE: "Honour thy father and thy mother." Mark 7:10a

TABLE ACTIVITY: Paint a Mother's Day card.

MATERIALS: Paint, paint brushes, white paper.

PROCEDURE: Allow children to paint their moms a special picture using their own creativity. When dry, write *Happy Mother's Day* somewhere on the picture.

DISCUSSION: What do you especially like to do with your mom? Do you like her to hug you? Play with you? Make you cookies? It's hard being a mommy. It's hard for a mom to know what to say when you're sad. It's hard for a mom to know whether or not to punish you if you've done something wrong. Mom's need to read their Bibles and pray so that they know how to be the best moms they can be. God helps them when they ask. Aren't you happy God helps your mom?

CIRCLE TIME ACTIVITIES
Recitation
L-O-V-E
Love is the best gift for me!

To the tune of "She'll Be Comin' 'Round the Mountain"

My mom's special as a mom can ever be.
My mom's special as a mom can ever be.
My mom's special and I love her,
She's so soft and warm and tender.
My mom's special as a mom can ever be.

To the tune of "This Old Man"

My mom comes and hugs me,
Then she puts me on her knee,
And she hugs me once and hugs me once again;
She's my very special friend.

Recitation
I know my mommy loves me so,
She prays for me where e'r I go.

To the tune of "Oh Be Careful"
Oh I am so glad my mom loves the Lord.
Oh I am so glad my mom loves the Lord.
She prays to Him each day,
Reads her Bible come what may;
Oh I am so glad my mom loves the Lord.

Recitation
Thank you, Lord, for giving me
A mother who is good to me.

Recitation
God gave my dear mom to me;
She makes me happy as can be.

SS896

'EAR THE WORD OF THE LORD

Matthew 11:15

Exodus 24:7b

Mark 12:30

John 3:16

James 4:8a

popcorn

leaf pattern

green construction paper

glue

'EAR THE WORD OF THE LORD is a fun board that utilizes the crafts the children make. The Bible verses that are displayed with the ears could be used for a discussion with older children. Once again, a bright background is appropriate here.

SS896

'EAR THE WORD OF THE LORD

PURPOSE: A fun board that allows children the opportunity to create a craft to complete the bulletin board display.

SUGGESTED BIBLE VERSE: "He that hath ears to hear, let him hear." Matthew 11:15

TABLE ACTIVITY: This table activity will be used to complete the display.

MATERIALS: Oaktag, pattern on page 81, glue, kernels of popped popcorn, slips of white paper (Bible verses), green construction paper (leaves).

PROCEDURE: Before class it will be necessary for the teacher to trace and cut out the ear of corn on oaktag. It may also be necessary for the teacher to cut out the leaf as well if the class is of a younger age group. During class time the children will glue pieces of popcorn to the *ears*. When finished they may be hung on the display.

DISCUSSION: Do you have ears? You do? What do you do with your ears? Our verse today tells us one way we can learn about the Bible. What does it tell us? (Reread the verse to the children.) Do you like hearing stories from the Bible? When we hear a story from the Bible we know it is true. How do we know it is true? We know because the Bible is the Word of God.

CIRCLE TIME ACTIVITIES

MUSICAL EARS: If you live in a rural community you may be able to obtain an ear of corn from a farmer or perhaps you can purchase one in the supermarket. If both of these options are impossible, take one of your craft ears and use it for this activity. Begin music. Pass the ear around. When the music stops, the one who has the ear must leave the circle. The child who is left wins the game. Treat everyone to some candy corn.

To the tune of "He's Got the Whole World in His Hands"

O let's listen to the Word.
O let's listen to God's Word.
O let's listen to the Word,
If you have ears, won't you hear?

To the tune of "London Bridge"

Hear God's word and you will learn,
You will learn, you will learn;
Hear God's word and you will learn,
What the Bible says.

Finger Play

Hear the Bible;
Listen well,
(hold hand to ear)
Then its stories you can tell.
(touch mouth)

Recitation

If you have ears, listen well,
Then what you learn, you can tell.

THIS IS THE DAY THAT THE LORD HAS MADE

How do we feel when we get up in the morning? THIS IS THE DAY THAT THE LORD HAS MADE is a display that encourages excitement with each new day. The happy sun reminds children to smile with each new morning. Bright yellows, oranges, purples and greens make this a cheerful addition to any classroom.

SS896

THIS IS THE DAY THAT THE LORD HAS MADE

PURPOSE: To help students realize that everyone has a bad day now and then, and that each new day offers a new beginning.

SUGGESTED BIBLE VERSE: "This is the day which the Lord hath made; we will rejoice and be glad in it." Psalm 118:24

TABLE ACTIVITY: Make bright Bible verse motivators.

MATERIALS: Oaktag, patterns on page 84, orange-yellow construction paper, glue, slips of paper that say *This is the day that the Lord has made.*

PROCEDURE: Prior to class, trace starburst and circles. In class, have students cut out starburst and circles and attach slips of paper to them with glue.

DISCUSSION: Have you ever had a day when nothing seemed to go right? How did it make you feel? Sometimes if we're tired our day goes badly. Bad days don't usually last long. The nice thing is each new morning brings a brand new day—a chance to start over. Listen carefully as I read some verses (II Corinthians 1:3,4 and James 1:2,3). What does the Bible tell us to do?

CIRCLE TIME ACTIVITIES

A Puppet Play or Skit

MOM:	Benny! It's time to get up!
BENNY:	I don't want to!
MOM:	Come on, Benny. Today will be fun.
BENNY:	I'm so tired.
NARRATOR:	Benny pulled the covers over his head and snuggled down to sleep a little longer. He heard what his mother said, but he was tired. *(A telephone rings.)*
MOM:	Benny, the telephone is for you!
BENNY:	For me? Oh, wow!
NARRATOR:	Benny ran down the stairs just as fast as he could.
BENNY:	Hello, hello.
GRANDPA:	Benny, this is your grandpa talking. How are you?
BENNY:	Grandpa! Grandpa!
GRANDPA:	I'm going to be coming through town today. How would you like to go fishing?
BENNY:	Fishing? Oh, yes, yes, yes!
NARRATOR:	When Benny hung up the phone, he remembered what his mom had said about the day being fun.
BENNY:	Lord, thank you for today. I love you, Lord!

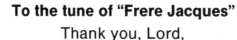

To the tune of "Frere Jacques"

Thank you, Lord,
Thank you, Lord,
For the fun you give me;
Thank you, heavenly Father,
Thank you, heavenly Father,
For the fun you give me.

SS896

WORSHIP HIS MAJESTY

leaves

Styrofoam packing "squiggles"

The beauty of God's creation invites us to WORSHIP HIS MAJESTY. This display is an easy way to illustrate beauty that only God can make. Use scenic calendar pictures on a light-blue or green background.

SS896

WORSHIP HIS MAJESTY

PURPOSE: To become conscious of the fact that the Lord created all things for us to enjoy.

SUGGESTED BIBLE VERSE: "And God saw every thing that he had made, and, behold, it was very good." Genesis 1:31a

TABLE ACTIVITY: Make a picture of a waterfall.

MATERIALS: Picture on page 85, Styrofoam packing "squiggles," glue, pre-cut green leaves from pattern on page 84.

PROCEDURE: Run off enough copies of the picture for each child in class. Glue pre-cut leaves to tree. Next, glue "squiggles" at the bottom of the waterfall to represent foam.

DISCUSSION: When you hear the word *creation*, what do you think of? Name some of the things God has made (Genesis 1). How do you feel about all God has made? How did God feel about all He had made (Genesis 1:31)?

CIRCLE TIME ACTIVITIES

Finger Play

God made the great big ocean;
(hands make a rippling horizontal motion)
God made the great big sky;
(throw hands into the air and wiggle fingers)
God made the pretty mountains
(make outline of mountains)
Much higher than you or I.
(point up, point to self)

To the tune of "Praise Him"

Praise Him, praise Him,
For the mighty mountains
High above, high above;
Praise Him, praise Him
For the mighty mountains,
High above, high above.

Praise Him, praise Him
For the tallest tree,
And the birds, and the birds;
Praise Him, praise Him
For the tallest tree,
And the birds, and the birds.

To the tune of "Deep and Wide"

Deep blue sea, deep blue sea,
Our God made the pretty, deep blue sea;
Deep blue sea, deep blue sea,
Our God made the pretty, deep blue sea.

Recitation

Jesus made what we can see,
He made it all for you and me.

SS896

I AM JESUS' LITTLE LAMB

I AM JESUS' LITTLE LAMB is the caption of this display that spotlights children. You will need a photograph of each child. Decorate with colorful construction paper flowers or place the child's craft under his picture for additional interest and emphasis.

 SS896

I AM JESUS' LITTLE LAMB

PURPOSE: To encourage children to be individuals. Each one is precious to God and He has a very special purpose for each of them.

SUGGESTED BIBLE VERSE: "I will praise thee; for I am fearfully and wonderfully made." Psalm 139:14a

TABLE ACTIVITY: Make cotton ball lambs.

MATERIALS: Pattern on page 86, oaktag, brightly colored construction paper, cotton balls, glue, markers, scissors.

PROCEDURE: Trace and cut out lamb. During class time children will be able to glue cotton balls onto their lambs. Write *I am Jesus' Little Lamb* on construction paper strips. Have children glue to the center of their lambs.

DISCUSSION: What is one thing that makes you different from anyone else? (Allow each child to respond.) Does Jesus know who you are? Did He make you special? How well does He know you? Are you important to Him? (Read Luke 12:6,7.)

CIRCLE TIME ACTIVITIES

Recitation

Little lambs love Jesus,
He thinks they are so sweet.
Who are Jesus' little lambs?
Each child upon the street.

Recitation

I am happy just to say,
Jesus loves me every day.

Recitation

Oh, yes I am, Jesus' lamb.

To the tune of "B-I-N-G-O"

God made me special as can be;
There's no one else like me-e.
I am not the same, I am not the same, I am not the same,
There's no one else like me.

To the tune of "Baa, Baa, Black Sheep"

I am Jesus' little precious lamb,
I'm His lamb, oh, yes I am.
He loves me and I love Him;
With His love I always win.
I am Jesus' little precious lamb;
I'm His lamb, oh, yes I am.

SS896

JESUS LOVES ME

JESUS LOVES ME is a display that can open a discussion about sin. It is important to remind children that God loves them no matter what they might have done. Be sure children understand the importance of confessing any wrongdoing to the Lord. For a three-dimensional effect, put a real rock in the boy's hand and a real rubber band on his sling shot.

Shining Star Publications, Copyright © 1991, A division of Good Apple

JESUS LOVES ME

PURPOSE: To point out that everyone is a sinner and that Jesus died on the cross to take away our sins.

SUGGESTED BIBLE VERSE: "For all have sinned, and come short of the glory of God." Romans 3:23

TABLE ACTIVITY: Make smiley faces and sad faces to demonstrate Bible verses.

MATERIALS: Paper, yarn (for hair), slips of paper, glue, pattern of child on page 86.

PROCEDURE: Trace pattern of child on both sides of the paper. Glue hair on both sides. Draw a sad face on one side, a smiley face on the other. Place paper strips with Bible verses written out on the appropriate side. (Bible verses: Romans 3:23 and I John 1:9.)

DISCUSSION: Boys and girls, do you know what the word *sin* means? Sin is when we do something we know is wrong. When we sin it makes Jesus sad. How can we get rid of our sin? I am going to read some verses. If you listen carefully I'm sure you will be able to answer the question. (Read I John 3:4, Psalm 51:1,2 and Romans 10:8,9.)

CIRCLE TIME ACTIVITIES

To the tune of "Old MacDonald"

When I'm bad it makes God sad,
I'll try to be good.
And when I'm good it makes God glad,
I'll try to be good.
Oh, I'll try, try, try, and I'll try, try, try;
I will try, I will try, every day I'll try, try.
When I'm bad it makes God sad,
I'll try to be good.

To the tune of "Row, Row, Row Your Boat"

Jesus loves me lots,
Even when I'm bad;
He loves me so very much,
Even when He's sad.

To the tune of "Skip to My Lou"

I will try and not do what's wrong.
I will try and not do what's wrong.
I will try and not do what's wrong;
I'll try to be good.
Try, try, I'll really try.
Try, try, I'll really try.
Try, try, I'll really try.
I'll try to be good.

JESUS LOVES THE LITTLE

CHILDREN OF THE WORLD

JESUS LOVES THE LITTLE CHILDREN is a display with a picture of a globe and some children. Use blue and green for the globe on a light-blue or light-gray background. The children should be of some nationalities not represented in your class.

 SS896

JESUS LOVES THE LITTLE CHILDREN OF THE WORLD

PURPOSE: To stress that Jesus loves all of the children in the world, not just the ones in our own nation, state or county.

SUGGESTED BIBLE VERSE: "Even so it is not the will of your Father which is in heaven, that one of these little ones should perish." Matthew 18:14

TABLE ACTIVITY: Make masks.

MATERIALS: Paper plates, crayons, yarn, paper punch, scraps of construction paper, glue.

PROCEDURE: Prior to class, cut eye, nose and mouth holes out of the plates. During class, let the children choose the color they want for their plates. Color and decorate. Punch holes and place yarn for ties.

DISCUSSION: Have you ever thought Jesus loved you more than someone else? Have you ever thought Jesus loved someone else more than you? Do you think Jesus loves children around the world though they may not know about Him? Do you think a child's skin color makes a difference to God? What do you think the word *perish* means in this verse?

CIRCLE TIME ACTIVITIES

To the tune of "Three Blind Mice"

Jesus loves. Jesus loves.
Isn't He good? Isn't He good?
He loves each one of us very much.
He loves to help us to live and such.
Jesus loves us very much;
He's good to us.

To the tune of "The Wise Man and the Foolish Man"

Jesus loves all the children of the world.
Jesus loves all the children of the world.
Jesus loves all the children of the world;
He-e loves them very much.
He loves them when they're good and when they're bad.
He loves them when they're good and when they're bad.
He loves them when they're good and when they're bad;
He loves them so very much.

To the tune of "Oh Be Careful"

Jesus loves all the children of the world,
Jesus loves all the children of the world;
If you're black or white or green,
Or anything between,
Jesus loves the little children of the world.

Recitation

Jesus loves the children,
Every single day;
He will always help them,
If they'll only pray.

SS896

I AM FEARFULLY AND WONDERFULLY MADE

No boys or girls are so identical that they even have the same personality. God made each one special. Nature has something that is individual also, the snowflake. I AM FEARFULLY AND WONDERFULLY MADE is a display that demonstrates the uniqueness of each child with that of a specific snowflake. The craft will be used to complete the display. Use a dark-blue background, light-blue lettering and quilt batting or cotton for the ground cover.

43 SS896

I AM FEARFULLY AND WONDERFULLY MADE

PURPOSE: To talk about each child being special in a different way; to focus on snowflakes which God also made different from each other.

SUGGESTED BIBLE VERSE: "I will praise thee; for I am fearfully and wonderfully made." Psalm 139:14a

TABLE ACTIVITY: Make snowflakes.

MATERIALS: White typing paper, glue, cotton, glitter, picture of each child.

PROCEDURE: Prior to class, cut out snowflakes. For less detail, fold into fourths. If a more special design is desired, fold accordingly. Precut pictures to desired size. During class time, allow children to glue little wisps of cotton on their snowflakes. Next they may add glitter. Finally, have the children glue their pictures to the centers of the snowflakes.

DISCUSSION: Look around the room. How many of you look exactly alike? Like the snowflakes, we are all different. Even twins, who look alike, are different in some ways. And sometimes God allows children to be born who can't walk or talk and some who can't think very well. He knew before they were born that they would be that way. It makes Him sad if we laugh or make fun of those who are different than we are. God loves us all very much! Isn't God good?

CIRCLE TIME ACTIVITIES

To the chorus of "Oh, Susanna"

Snowflakes come in many different shapes;
Oh, I love to see the snowflakes come
When winter takes its place.

To the tune of "Frere Jacques"

See the snow.
See the snow.
See it fall.
See it fall.
It comes tumbling down.
It comes tumbling down;
To the ground, to the ground.

Recitation

God made snowflakes
God made me;
We are special
Can't you see?

Recitation

Snowflakes fall from up above,
Reminding me of God's great love.

SS896

FAITH OF OUR FATHERS

What is more special than a day spent with a godly father? FAITH OF OUR FATHERS is a display that shows a father and son fishing. Include a Bible on the bank. Use the colors of your choice for this display. For fun, use an old tree branch for the fishing pole and put a smile on the faces of the fish.

 SS896

FAITH OF OUR FATHERS

PURPOSE: To talk about our earthly father's love and our heavenly Father's love.

SUGGESTED BIBLE VERSE: "Hear, ye children, the instruction of a father." Proverbs 4:1a

TABLE ACTIVITY: Make a gift for Dad.

MATERIALS: Tagboard, various colors of construction paper, bow tie pattern on page 87, macaroni of various shapes and sizes.

PROCEDURE: Prior to class, make pattern and trace tie onto paper. When it's time for the activity, have the children glue the macaroni to the tie. Write *Happy Father's Day* on the bottom.

DISCUSSION: Do you ever do fun things with your dad? Dads can be pretty special people, but there's a Father who is more special than any other dad. God is our heavenly Father, and He loves us very much! Our Bible words today tell us we should listen to our father. God, our Father, teaches us things in the Bible. We can learn what the Bible says by going to Sunday school and church and listening when someone reads from the Bible. I'm glad God has a way to tell us what to do.

CIRCLE TIME ACTIVITIES

To the tune of "Mary Had a Little Lamb"

My God is so good to me,
Good to me,
Good to me;
My God is so good to me,
And I love Him so.

Recitation

I love Dad and he loves me,
We both love God especially!

To the tune of "I've Been Working on the Railroad"

I love God who is so tender,
He's like a dad to me;
I love God who is so tender,
He's just like a dad to me;
He loves me and He protects me,
Every single day of the year;
I love God who is tender,
And he loves me, too.
Oh yes, I love God.
Oh yes, I love God.
He is like a dad to me, to me;
Oh yes, I love God.
Oh yes, I love God.
He is like a dad to me.

SS896

OUR COUNTRY!

OUR COUNTRY! How wonderful it is to live in OUR COUNTRY! How important it is for children to learn how special our flag is. If you live in America the simplicity of this display will be especially effective if you use a light-blue background and bright red, white and blue for the flag. Tinfoil can be used for the lettering with a dark-blue shadow. For a border, consider red, white and blue stars. For an added touch, hang stars from the ceiling. (If you live in another country, use your own country's flag.)

SS896

OUR COUNTRY!

PURPOSE: To teach respect for our flag.

SUGGESTED BIBLE VERSE: "He rules forever by his power, his eyes watch the nations." Psalm 66:7a NIV

TABLE ACTIVITY: Make a flag.

MATERIALS: American flag pattern from page 88, square of blue paper, glue, sticky stars, colors.

PROCEDURE: (Please use your own country's flag. For an American flag, follow these directions.) Older children may be able to cut out the square. Younger children will need to have theirs done for them. Run off enough copies of the flag pattern for each child. Enlarge if desired. Have children glue blue background in proper place. Color strips (red) and glue in place. Allow children to stick some stars on the blue background.

DISCUSSION: Have you ever noticed what people do at a parade when the flag comes by? Some people stand. Some people put their hands over their hearts. If someone is wearing a hat, he will usually take it off. This is called *respect* for our flag. That's a big word, isn't it? When we see our flag, it reminds us that we live in the greatest country in the world. Our Country!

CIRCLE TIME ACTIVITIES

To the tune of "The B-I-B-L-E"

I love the flag I see,
It makes me hap-happy;
I'm glad I live in America,
I love the flag I see.

To the tune of "Fishers of Men"

Stand up when you see our flag come,
See our flag come,
See our flag come;
Stand up when you see our flag come,
It's a grand old flag.
It's a grand old flag,
It's a grand old flag;
Stand up when you see our flag come,
It's a grand old flag.

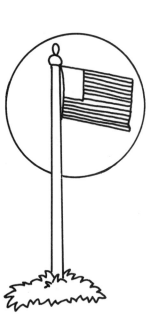

To the tune of "B-I-N-G-O"

I love the flag; I am so glad I am American.
I love our dear flag.
I love our dear flag.
I love our dear flag.
I am American.

To the tune of "Oh Be Careful"

Oh I love the good ol' red, white and blue.
Oh I love the good ol' red, white and blue.
When I see our big flag come,
I'm a proud American;
Oh I love the good ol' red, white and blue.

SS896

THY FAITHFULNESS IS TO ALL GENERATIONS

God did many wonderful things for people in Bible times. It is important for us to teach children of God's faithfulness throughout all of the years. THY FAITHFULNESS IS TO ALL GENERATIONS is a display which shows a grandfather, grandmother and a little child reading a Bible. Make Grandma's hair silver—Grandpa's, too. Pipe cleaners make interesting glasses. Use the colors of your choice for the rest of the board. A border of Bibles could be used, or the word *Faith* could surround the display.

SS896

THY FAITHFULNESS IS TO ALL GENERATIONS

PURPOSE: To point out to children that God helped people not only in Bible times, but He will help us now and in the future, as well.

SUGGESTED BIBLE VERSE: "Thy faithfulness is unto all generations." Psalms 119:90a

TABLE ACTIVITY: Plant a seed for an older adult.

MATERIALS: Styrofoam cups, potting soil, flower seeds, craft stickers, markers.

PROCEDURE: Decorate cups with markers. Plant flower seeds. Put the Bible verse on a craft stick and place it in the soil. Reproduce the following rhyme and glue it to the cup.

> See the little flower grow,
> God is faithful, this we know.
> Watch and care for tenderly,
> And when you see it, think of me.

DISCUSSION: Do you remember some of the stories in the Bible where God helped the people? What are some of your favorites? Have you ever heard your grandma or grandpa tell of times God helped them? Has God ever helped your mom and dad? Has He ever helped you? God's been around a long, long time helping people. He's also going to be with us forever. If we love Him and want Him as our best friend, we will live with Him forever.

CIRCLE TIME ACTIVITIES

To the tune of "Three Blind Mice"

God helped Noah.
God helped Noah.
Build an ark.
Build an ark.
God helped him build it, He'll help us too,
To do the things that we all should do.
God will help if we ask Him to;
Our God will help.

To the tune of "This Old Man"

God helps us.
God helps us.
Every day our God helps us.
He helps us all to live for Him each day.
God helps us in every way.

Recitation

God helps Grandma, God helps me,
God helps everyone you see.

SS896

WHO-O-O
LOVES YOU?
JESUS!

red construction paper

glue

craft feathers

If you want a fall display that children can help create, WHO-O-O LOVES YOU? JESUS! is for you. The owls made by the children for the table activity may be hung beside the big owl. Craft feathers will add color and texture to this board.

SS896

WHO-O-O LOVES YOU? JESUS!

PURPOSE: To remind children that Jesus loves them.

SUGGESTED BIBLE VERSE: "God is love." I John 4:16b

TABLE ACTIVITY: This craft activity will complete the display.

MATERIALS: Pattern of owl found on page 86, glue, red construction paper, colorful craft feathers.

PROCEDURE: Prior to class, make owl pattern and trace onto a sheet of paper as a master copy. Run off enough copies for all children. Cut out small hearts for the children to glue onto the chests of the owls. During class time each child may glue the craft feathers and a heart onto his owl. When dry, place on a bulletin board.

DISCUSSION: How do we know Jesus loves us? In Bible times Jesus showed His love by making sick people well, by feeding the hungry and by doing other great things. What is the biggest way Jesus has shown His love for us? How can we show our love to Him?

CIRCLE TIME ACTIVITIES

Finger Play

Who-o-o loves you?
(point to each other)
Jesus loves me.
(point to self)
Who-o-o?
Jesus!
(point to sky)
Who-o-o?
Jesus!
(point to sky)

A March
To the tune of "Jesus Loves Me"

Have children flap their arms like wings, and

Sing "Whooo, Whooo, Whooo" to the tune. When the song is over, have them yell JESUS!

Recitation

The wise old owl just told me
A very special thought;
He told me Jesus loves me,
Not a little, but a lot.

To the tune of "Deep and Wide"

Who loves you? Who loves you?
It is Jesus, this is really true;
Who loves you? Who loves you?
It is Jesus, this is really true.

Recitation

My big God lives in heaven above;
He looks on me with special love.

SS896

TO EVERYTHING THERE IS A SEASON is a display that portrays the different seasons using squirrels as the focus. Spring—babies; summer—growth; fall—harvest and preparation; winter—rest. For a three-dimensional effect, add fur or homemade pom-poms anywhere a squirrel is displayed. Or, put a half of a walnut shell on the place where the squirrel is shown holding a nut. A border of walnut halves would also be cute. Because squirrels are not as colorful as some of God's creation, use a bright, colorful background.

SS896

TO EVERYTHING THERE IS A SEASON

PURPOSE: To teach children that in God's plan, each season has a purpose.

SUGGESTED BIBLE VERSE: "To every thing there is a season, and a time to every purpose under the heaven." Ecclesiastes 3:1

TABLE ACTIVITY: Make a seasonal picture.

MATERIALS: Crayons, picture on page 89, glue, small brown craft pom-poms (baby squirrel—spring), green construction paper, scissors (fringe for grass—summer), one-half of a walnut shell (place in squirrels paw—fall), cotton (glue around tree trunk for snow—winter).

PROCEDURE: Reproduce enough pictures for all class members. Glue respective articles to places indicated. Color pictures.

DISCUSSION: Do you know what a season is? It's a certain time of year. Our year is made up of four seasons—spring, summer, fall, and winter. Who made the seasons? God planned the seasons so that different things happen at different times. For example, in the spring, animals have babies. In the summer, they live, grow and play. In the fall, some animals begin to store food for winter when they sleep the season away. God's plan includes new life, growth, harvest and rest. Isn't God good?

SEASONS NEWS REPORT

(Children can pantomime, holding a picture of the animal they represent.)

This is Sachel Squirrel reporting to you from station T-R-E-E. What a lovely spring day this is. The trees are budding and a few tulips are beginning to bloom. What causes the seasons? I'm going to ask this important question of some experts in the field. Miss Mouse, I see you are scampering to and fro. Do you know who made the seasons?

M.M.: No, I don't know who made them. Why don't you ask Grover Groundsquirrel?

S.S.: Grover Groundsquirrel? Why, he's a cousin of mine. Why didn't I think of him? Grover! Grover! Can you tell me who made the seasons?

G.G.: No, I don't know who made the seasons. Why don't you ask Ollie Owl? She should know.

S.S.: Ollie Owl, are you up there?

O.O.: Wh-o-o-o's calling?

S.S.: It's me, Sachel Squirrel. Can you tell me who made the seasons?

O.O.: Of course I can! I'm a wise old owl. God made the seasons. He made each one just right. He made all of the seasons with all of His great might. The Bible says in Ecclesiastes 3:1 that there is a time for every purpose under heaven. That means God made each season for a special purpose. Each season needs the others to function properly.

S.S.: Thank you, Ollie Owl. You truly are wise. Well, there you have it, folks. This is Sachel Squirrel signing off from station T-R-E-E. Goodnight everyone.

To the tune of "Twinkle, Twinkle, Little Star"

Our God makes the seasons come;
He helps them come one by one.
He helps things to live and grow.
He makes all things, this I know.
Our God makes the seasons come;
He helps them come one by one.

SS896

COME YE THANKFUL PEOPLE

movable eyes · glue · yarn · craft sticks · Come ye thankful people

Kids love toys! COME YE THANKFUL PEOPLE is a fun board which encourages children to look at their playthings as gifts from God. Use a variety of colors for this display. For a three-dimensional effect, yarn can be glued on the children for hair.

Shining Star Publications, Copyright © 1991, A division of Good Apple SS896

COME YE THANKFUL PEOPLE

PURPOSE: To encourage children to realize their playthings come from God.

SUGGESTED BIBLE VERSE: "So we thy people . . . will give thee thanks for ever." Psalm 79:13a

TABLE ACTIVITY: Make a stick horse.

MATERIALS: Enlarged patterns from page 90, black marker, brightly colored construction paper, movable eyes, glue, yarn (cut in 2″ pieces for mane), craft sticks.

PROCEDURE: Trace around pattern using black marker. Allow children to glue on yarn and eyes to both sides of the horse, then add a craft stick to the back of one and glue sides together. It would be helpful to have a sample already made.

DISCUSSION: What is your favorite toy? Did you know that toys come from God? They do. Our toys are made out of things God created. God helps our moms and dads and grandmas and grandpas make money so they can buy us toys. Isn't God good?

CIRCLE TIME ACTIVITIES

To the tune of "Skip to My Lou"

God helped me get toys that I have.
God helped me get toys that I have.
God helped me get toys that I have.
Thank you, God, for helping.
Thank you for my neat toys.
Thank you for my neat toys.
Thank you for my neat toys.
Thank you, God, for helping.

To the tune of "London Bridge"

God helps my folks give me toys,
Give me toys,
Give me toys.
God helps my folks give me toys;
Thank you, God, for helping.

To the tune of "Old MacDonald"

Thank you, Lord, for all my toys
You have given me;
They make me hap-hap-hap-happy,
Thank you for my toys.
I'll say thanks, thanks, thanks.
I'll say thanks, thanks, thanks.
Thank you, Lord, for my toys.
I just praise and thank you.
Thank you, Lord, for all my toys;
Thank you, thank you, Lord.

Recitation
T-O-Y-S
Does God give me toys? YES!

GOD GIVES US ALL THINGS TO ENJOY

Every child has something he or she enjoys. GOD GIVES US ALL THINGS TO ENJOY is a display that shows children enjoying nonmaterial blessings in a variety of situations. A number of materials may be used to give the board a three-dimensional effect. For example, yarn could be used for ropes on the swing, fringed black construction paper could be used for the eyelashes of the praying child, and movable eyes could be used on the family.

GOD GIVES US ALL THINGS TO ENJOY

PURPOSE: To encourage children to think about the things we take for granted; those that aren't material in nature.

SUGGESTED BIBLE VERSE: "Every good gift and every perfect gift is from above." James 1:17a

TABLE ACTIVITY: Make a collage.

MATERIALS: Construction paper (size and color of your choice), catalogs, family and outdoor magazines, glue, scissors.

PROCEDURE: Each child may tear or cut out items that he enjoys from a catalog or magazine. Encourage them to choose things like outdoors or families—things that are felt or observed, not possessed. Glue to paper.

DISCUSSION: Do any of you like Christmas and birthdays? Why? (Children will mention presents, cake, etc., of course.) Do you know God gives us presents every day? They aren't presents like our moms and dads give us. God gives us presents like rain, sunshine, family and friends. He gives us presents that can't be wrapped. I'm so thankful for the presents God gives me, aren't you?

CIRCLE TIME ACTIVITIES

To the tune of "The Wise Man and the Foolish Man"

I thank you, Lord, for all the things you give.
I thank you, Lord, for all the things you give.
I thank you, Lord, for all the things you give;
For the big outdoors, thank you, Lord.
For the big outdoors, I thank you, oh my Lord.
For the big outdoors, I thank you, oh my Lord.
For the big outdoors, I thank you, oh my Lord;
Thank you for the things you give.

Second verse—For my friends so dear
Third verse—For my mom and dad
Fourth verse—For my faith in you

To the tune of "Three Blind Mice"

God gives things, to enjoy.
Let's thank the Lord.
Let's thank the Lord.
We thank you, Lord, for all things today.
We thank you, Lord, for all you send our way.
Thanks for loving us come what may.
Let's thank the Lord.

Recitation

Thank you, Lord, for all you do;
We know you love us, this is true.

SS896

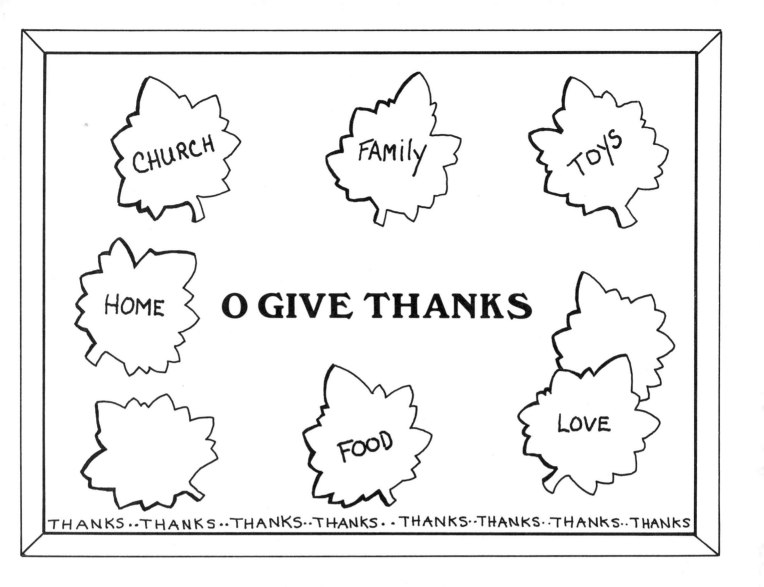

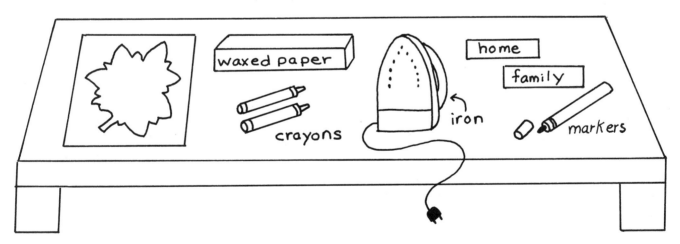

O GIVE THANKS is a more traditional display that can be used at Thanksgiving. Big maple leaves feature words of different things we should be thankful for. Orange, red and brown leaves can be used on this display. For added interest, a border of *Thanks* could be used. To accomplish this, use 2" wide strips of a contrasting paper. Write *Thanks*, in marker, over and over. Place around the display.

O GIVE THANKS

PURPOSE: To focus on things we should be thankful for and to learn to recognize them.

SUGGESTED BIBLE VERSE: "O give thanks unto the Lord, for he is good." Psalm 136:1a

TABLE ACTIVITY: Make splattered leaves.

MATERIALS: Leaf pattern on page 91, oaktag, crayons, scissors, waxed paper, iron, typing paper.

PROCEDURE: Prior to class, trace and cut out leaves. Instruct children to color *heavily* on their leaves. Cover with waxed paper. Using a warm iron, iron over the waxed paper. The leaves should have a splattered look to them. Peel off paper. Ask each child to name something he is thankful for. Write it on a slip of paper and glue it to the leaf.

DISCUSSION: What kinds of things should we be thankful for? Should we only be thankful for the good things God gives us? Why or why not? I'm going to read some verses. Listen carefully to what they say. The Bible helps us know what to be thankful for. (Read James 1:2,3 and Colossians 3:17.)

CIRCLE TIME ACTIVITIES

To the tune of "Jesus Loves Me"

We will give our thanks to God.
We will give our thanks to God.
We will thank Him everyday,
For the things He sends our way.
Yes, we'll give thanks.
Yes, we'll give thanks.
Yes, we'll give thanks.
Give thanks unto our God.

To the tune of "Skip to My Lou"

Oh give thanks to God up above.
Oh give thanks to God up above.
Oh give thanks to God up above.
Our God is so good.
Give thanks, won't you give thanks?
Give thanks, won't you give thanks?
Give thanks, won't you give thanks?
Give all your thanks to God.

To the tune of "The B-I-B-L-E"

Give thanks in all you do,
And our God will bless you.
Just sing a song to the Lord today;
Give thanks in all you do.

SS896

A MIGHTY FORTRESS IS OUR GOD

Who protects us when we're afraid? God does. A MIGHTY FORTRESS IS OUR GOD is a fun board that displays one of the joys of winter. Use a dark-blue background and white construction paper "blocks." Dress the children in bright winter colors. Use quilt batting or cotton for the ground cover of snow.

A MIGHTY FORTRESS IS OUR GOD

PURPOSE: To discuss with children the protective power of God.

SUGGESTED BIBLE VERSE: "The Lord is the strength of my life; of whom shall I be afraid?" Psalm 27:1b

TABLE ACTIVITY: Build a "snow fort" out of sugar cubes and frosting.

MATERIALS: Sugar cubes, frosting, heavy cardboard, slips of paper, colored pipe cleaners, toothpicks.

PROCEDURE: According to the size of the class, determine how big each snow fort will be. Perhaps you will want to make one big fort instead of individual ones. When you have determined the size of the fort(s), cut cardboard for the base. If each child will be doing an individual project, have the cubes divided equally in plastic bags for easy distribution. The frosting is to be the "glue" between the cubes. A pipe cleaner cross may be added to the top of the fort. When the projects are completed, write *A Mighty Fortress Is Our God* on slips of paper and fasten to toothpicks like a flag. Secure in the location deemed appropriate by each child.

DISCUSSION: Do you like to play in the snow? It's fun, isn't it? Have you ever made a snow fort? If you have, you know you can hide behind it. When someone throws snowballs at you, they can't hit you if you're behind the fort. God keeps us safe just like a fort protects us from snowballs.

CIRCLE TIME ACTIVITIES

To the tune of "Oh, Susanna"

Oh, my God is strong as He can be;
He keeps me from all harm.
I can't see Him but I know He's there;
He keeps me from all harm.
My God's strong.
He's strong as He can be.
He keeps me from all harm, you see;
He's strong as He can be.

Recitation

When I'm scared, my God is near;
When I pray I know He'll hear.

Recitation

God is everywhere I go;
He is with me, this I know.

Action Rhyme

My God is strong!
(show your muscles)
He keeps me from all harm.
He protects me everyday,
With His great big loving arms.
(wrap arms around self)

SS896

O COME, LET US ADORE HIM

O COME, LET US ADORE HIM is a display that gives a modern setting to the appearance of the Christmas star. For this display, bright Christmas colors are most effective. Dark midnight blue for the sky, gold foil wrapping paper for the star, and white cotton for the snow are the basics. Work red and green into the rest of the scene. Depending on the size of the board, real garland could be placed on the Christmas tree.

SS896

O COME, LET US ADORE HIM

PURPOSE: To demonstrate through childlike wonder the joy of adoring Jesus.

SUGGESTED BIBLE VERSE: "And when they were come into the house, they saw the young child with Mary his mother, and fell down, and worshipped him." Matthew 2:11a

TABLE ACTIVITY: Make babies wrapped in swaddling clothes.

MATERIALS: Pattern of baby Jesus on page 92, roll of gauze bandage cut in strips, glue, crayons.

PROCEDURE: Run off enough copies of the baby Jesus for each child. Next, allow each child to glue strips of gauze to the baby's body to represent swaddling clothes. Children may color the picture if they desire.

DISCUSSION: What does it mean to adore Jesus? I'm going to read what the dictionary says the word means. What are some gifts we can give? Listen very carefully as I read some verses. I'm sure you will hear some clues. (Read Matthew 25:35-40, Mark 8:38 and John 15:10.)

CIRCLE TIME ACTIVITIES

To the tune of "Jesus Loves Me"

Jesus came at Christmastime.
Jesus came at Christmastime.
Jesus came at Christmastime.
He came as a little babe.
Yes, Jesus came. Yes, Jesus came.
Yes, Jesus came;
The Bible tells me so.

To the tune of "O Come, All Ye Faithful"

O come, let us adore Him.
O come, let us adore Him.
O come, let us adore Him, Christ, the Lord.

To the tune of "He's Got the Whole World in His Hands"

My Jesus had a bed of hay.
My Jesus laid His head upon the hay.
My Jesus had a bed of hay,
Where He could lay His little head.

Recitation

Tiny Baby on the hay,
You came here on Christmas Day.

Recitation

Jesus came to earth below,
So His love we all could know.

SS896

JOY TO THE WORLD

Christmas is a special time. A time for joy, love and family. JOY TO THE WORLD is a display showing a house and church. At Christmas the church and home become especially dear. Use a dark-blue background and white quilt batting or cotton for snow. Use colors of your choice for the church, home and lettering.

SS896

JOY TO THE WORLD

PURPOSE: To talk about different ways people can find joy, especially focusing on family and church traditions.

SUGGESTED BIBLE VERSE: "Therefore, brethren, stand fast, and hold the traditions which ye have been taught." II Thessalonians 2:15a

TABLE ACTIVITY: Make a food basket.

MATERIALS: Fruit, canned goods, baked goods, nuts, a basket, a big bow, white typing paper, scraps of construction paper, glue, markers.

PROCEDURE: Have each child sign up to bring a specific item that will be used to make a food basket for someone in need. Cut various shapes out of construction paper prior to class. Using white typing paper, let the children arrange the shapes onto the paper to make a card. Inside, write the simple message: *Joy to the World.* Have the children sign their cards. Take the food basket and cards to someone who could use some cheer.

DISCUSSION: Do you know what the word *joy* means? It's another word for happiness. One way we can feel happy at Christmas is to have traditions. Do you know what a tradition is? That's a long word for something you do year after year. Some churches have the *tradition* of taking food baskets to people in need. Some churches have the *tradition* of having church on Christmas Eve. Families can have traditions, as well. Perhaps your family has certain food they eat every Christmas. Or, maybe you have a certain way you open your presents. Traditions, whether done in church or at home, bring joy to people.

CIRCLE TIME ACTIVITIES

Recitation
Christmas is a time for joy,
For every little girl and boy.

Recitation
I am small but I can say,
"Have a joyful Christmas Day."

To the tune of "The Farmer in the Dell"
Oh, Christmas brings us joy.
Oh, Christmas brings us joy.
I'm so glad that Jesus came;
Oh, Christmas brings us joy.

To the tune of "Mary Had a Little Lamb"
Christmas brings us joy each year;
Joy each year,
Joy each year;
Christmas brings us joy each year;
Thank you, Lord, for Christmas.

SS896

O HOLY NIGHT

Have you ever wondered what the animals did the night Jesus was born? Did they just stand there, or could they sense the holiness of the moment? O HOLY NIGHT is a bulletin board that gives the sense of wonder one likes to imagine the animals experienced. Fur manes and cotton may be added for a three-dimensional effect. Real hay or shredded yellow paper may be put around the top of the manger. Using a dark midnight blue background will give a nighttime appearance.

Shining Star Publications, Copyright © 1991, A division of Good Apple

SS896

O HOLY NIGHT

PURPOSE: To impress upon children the lowliness of the manger.

SUGGESTED BIBLE VERSE: ". . .she . . . laid him in a manger; because there was no room for them in the inn." Luke 2:7

TABLE ACTIVITY: Make a manger scene.

MATERIALS: Enlarged, reproduced copies of the display, craft sticks, glue, shredded yellow paper, fur or cotton if desired.

PROCEDURE: Run enough copies for each child to make a manger scene. Shred yellow paper (yellow typing paper would work well). Let children glue on craft sticks, shredded paper, fur and cotton.

DISCUSSION: Where were you born? Most people are born in a hospital. Jesus was born in a stable. That's another word for a barn. There was no room in a nearby motel, so the manager told Mary and Joseph they could sleep in the stable. Because Mary didn't have a crib for Jesus, she laid Him in a manger. A manger is a part of the barn where animals eat.

CIRCLE TIME ACTIVITIES
A Puppet Play

CHARACTERS: Animal puppets. If you don't have the types of animals suggested, change the names in the story.

OSCAR OX:	Hey! What's that noise? It sounds like people coming.
DEXTER DONKEY:	It sure does. It sounds like they're getting closer and closer.
LITTLE LAMB:	I hear a lady's voice. It sounds like she's very tired. She's riding on a little donkey. Oh, my goodness! It looks like she's going to have a baby!
OSCAR OX:	Having a baby and she's coming here?
LITTLE LAMB:	Sh-h-h. It sounds like the innkeeper. He's telling them there's no room for them in the inn, but that they're welcome to stay here.
DEXTER DONKEY:	Oh, dear. I sure hope the baby doesn't decide to be born while they're here!
LITTLE LAMB:	Don't be silly, Dexter. No baby should be born in a stable.
DEXTER DONKEY:	Well, I'll still feel better when morning comes and they're on their way.
NARRATOR:	All the animals agreed—it would be better if the baby was born somewhere other than the stable. Many things were running through the animals' minds that night. Finally, they were able to go to sleep. Very early the next morning they were awakened by an unfamiliar sound.
OSCAR OX:	What's that noise?
DEXTER DONKEY:	I don't know, Oscar.
LITTLE LAMB:	You silly guys, it's a baby. The Baby was born last night! Don't the parents look happy?
DEXTER DONKEY:	I wonder if we could take a look?
OSCAR OX:	Do we dare?
LITTLE LAMB:	Let's try.
NARRATOR:	So Oscar Ox, Dexter Donkey and Little Lamb inched their way to the manger. When they looked inside, they knew that Baby was special. Now it didn't matter that they hadn't wanted the Baby to be born that night. When they looked at Him, they felt the warmth of His love. And that's the best feeling of all.

SS896

How did the shepherds find out about Jesus' birth? An angel told them. GLORIA! is a display that features Christmas tree garland and angels to make its Christmas statement. In the center of the board, on dark-blue construction paper, trace the word *GLORIA*. Glue or staple the garland around the lettering. Next, place angels that are made out of white paper around the word. For additional appeal, add angels to your ceiling. (See an angel pattern on page 91.)

GLORIA!

PURPOSE: To focus on the special announcement of Jesus' birth.

SUGGESTED BIBLE VERSE: "Glory to God in the highest, and on earth peace, good will toward men." Luke 2:14

TABLE ACTIVITIES: Make glittering Gloria's.

MATERIALS: A large sheet of dark-blue paper for each child, glue, glitter, white crayon.

PROCEDURE: Before class, write *Gloria* in white crayon on dark-blue paper. Help children outline the letters in glue. Children may sprinkle with glitter. Gloria!

DISCUSSION: When you were born, how did your parents tell others? Some examples are: phone calls, sending birth announcements, or putting it in the paper. When Jesus was born, do you think Mary and Joseph phoned the shepherds to tell them about the Baby Jesus? Do you think they sent them a pretty announcement? I know, maybe they put it in the Bethlehem Daily Newspaper. You don't think so? Well, if they didn't tell the shepherds like that, how did they tell them? They didn't tell them! An angel did! That seems funny, doesn't it. First, one angel told them and then many angels joined in singing, "Glory to God in the highest, and on earth, peace, good will toward men."

CIRCLE TIME ACTIVITIES

Recitation

"Gloria," the angel sang;
I'm so glad that Jesus came.

Recitation

I am happy as can be,
Jesus came to earth for me!

To the tune of "She'll Be Comin' 'Round the Mountain"

Oh, the angels sang loud glor-i-as that night.
Oh, the angels sang loud glor-i-as that night.
Oh, the angels, they sang, "Gloria."
Oh, the angels, they sang, "Gloria."
Oh, the angels sang loud glor-i-as that night.

To the tune of "Baa, Baa, Black Sheep"

"Gloria," all the angels sang that night,
As they gleamed with bright, bright, light.
"Gloria, Gloria," they all sang.
"Gloria, Gloria," they all sang.
"Gloria," all the angels sang that night,
As they gleamed with bright, bright light.

Recitation

Gloria! Gloria!
Glory to God in the highest!
Gloria! Gloria!
Glory to God in the highest!

WE THREE KINGS

Who were the most colorful characters in the Christmas nativity? The wise men. WE THREE KINGS is a display that demonstrates a part of their participation in the Christmas story. Rich royal colors are a must for this display. Royal blue, purple, gold and silver make a striking impression. For the background, use a medium gray or light blue. For crowns, use gold or silver wrapping paper. Craft beads may be used for jewels. A bright-yellow star is all that's needed to complete this display.

SS896

WE THREE KINGS

PURPOSE: To talk about how the wise men used their wealth as a form of worship for Jesus and how we can too.

SUGGESTED BIBLE VERSE: ". . .they presented unto him gifts; gold, frankincense, and myrrh." Matthew 2:11b

TABLE ACTIVITY: Make a treasure box.

MATERIALS: Kitchen matchboxes (enough for each child to have one), light-brown construction paper, old jewelry, buttons or craft beads, glue, candy jewelry.

PROCEDURE: Using light-brown construction paper, measure and cut rectangles measuring 4¾" x 8¾". It is important that the children do not cut these out due to the need for accuracy. Help children glue the paper to the hollow part of the box. Let dry for a little while. Next, have the children glue on the jewels. When everything is dry, fill with candy jewelry. A gift fit for a king (or queen).

DISCUSSION: Do you know anyone who has lots of money? How do they spend their money? The wise men were very rich. They used some of their money to buy special presents for the baby Jesus. This was their way of worshipping Him. When we give some of our money to the church, it makes God very happy. Do you know that the very best gift you can give God is yourself? That's right. He wants you to love Him more than He wants any of the money you might have.

CIRCLE TIME ACTIVITIES

To the tune of "I've Been Working on the Railroad"

Wise men brought their gifts to Jesus,
On that special night;
Wise men brought their gifts to Jesus,
On that special night.
They were glad to see the Baby;
He was the Son of God.
Wise men brought their gifts to Jesus.
Wise men brought their gifts.
Wise men brought their gifts.
Wise men brought their gifts.
Wise men brought their gifts to Je-e-sus.
Wise men brought their gifts.
Wise men brought their gifts.
Wise men brought their gifts to Him.

To the tune of "The Wise Man and the Foolish Man"

The wise men brought their gifts to the Babe.
The wise men brought their gifts to the Babe.
The wise men brought their gifts to the Babe,
From their homeland far away.
They brought their gifts to Him on that special night.
They brought their gifts to Him on that special night.
They brought their gifts to Him on that special night.
Wise men brought their gifts to the Lord.

Recitation

What can I give the Christ child?
Me!

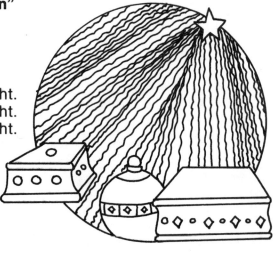

 SS896

JESUS IS THE REASON

With all the hustle and bustle of Christmas, we sometimes forget the real reason we celebrate the season. JESUS IS THE REASON is a display with a secular scene and a christian message. For a three-dimensional effect, use felt for the stockings and fringed green construction paper for the tree.

  SS896

JESUS IS THE REASON

PURPOSE: To stress to children that the reason we celebrate Christmas is Jesus.

SUGGESTED BIBLE VERSE: "For unto us a child is born." Isaiah 9:6a

TABLE ACTIVITY: Make stocking-shaped reminders.

MATERIALS: Stocking pattern from page 93, red felt or red construction paper, quilt batting or cotton, glue, written messages: *Jesus Is the Reason*.

PROCEDURE: Trace around pattern. Older children may be able to cut out stocking. It will need to be done for younger children. Mark an *X* on the heel, toe and along the top where you will want the children to glue the batting or cotton. Pass out the messages so the children can glue them onto the stocking.

DISCUSSION: What do you like best about Christmas? (Most children will say presents.) Who was born on Christmas? Jesus is the reason we give presents, sing, and go to church at Christmas. Christmas is a happy time. It reminds us of Jesus.

CIRCLE TIME ACTIVITIES

To the tune of "Mary Had a Little Lamb"

Jesus is just why we sing,
Why we sing,
Why we sing;
Jesus is just why we sing,
During Christmastime.

To the tune of "Here We Go 'Round the Mulberry Bush"

When we have Christmas, it's for Him.
It's for Him.
It's for Him.
When we have Christmas, it's for Him;
It's for our dear Jesus.

To the tune of "Jesus Loves the Little Ones Like Me, Me, Me"

Jesus came at Christmastime for me, me, me.
Jesus came at Christmastime for me, me, me.
Came to earth for me,
He came so willingly;
Jesus came at Christmastime for me, me, me.

Jesus came at Christmastime for you, you, you.
Jesus came at Christmastime for you, you, you.
Came to earth for you,
He loves you through and through;
Jesus came at Christmastime for you, you, you.

Recitation

Jesus is the reason, they say,
So let's remember Him this Christmas Day.

SS896

THERE'S A SONG IN THE AIR

THERE'S A SONG IN THE AIR is a display showing one of the aspects of Christmas. For a fun board, use pom-poms on the caroler's hat. If you knit or crochet, you could add light-weight neck scarves to the carolers. Bright Christmas colors are appropriate here. The songbook could be made from silver or gold wrapping paper.

 SS896

THERE'S A SONG IN THE AIR

PURPOSE: To learn the origin of a familiar Christmas hymn.

SUGGESTED BIBLE VERSE: "Sing, O heavens; and be joyful, O earth." Isaiah 49:13a

TABLE ACTIVITY: Make a Christmas tape.

MATERIALS: Tape recorder, a blank tape, children's voices, practice.

PROCEDURE: Make a tape of Christmas songs. Let the children listen to their "song in the air." If some of the children live away from their grandparents, it might be fun to send them a copy. Alternate activity: Have your class "carol" some of the other classes.

DISCUSSION: One of the nicest things about Christmas is the music. Do you have any favorite Christmas songs? I like "Away in a Manger." Let's sing it right now. There's a Christmas song you probably have heard, "O Little Town of Bethelehem." This song was written for children to sing. The author loved children, and because he loved the children of his church, he wanted to do something special for them. He wrote the words to the song and another man wrote the music. When Christmas day came, the children sang the song. Now, not only children, but adults love to sing the song, as well.

CIRCLE TIME ACTIVITIES

To the tune of "Row, Row, Row Your Boat"

Sing, sing, sing a song,
Sing at Christmastime.
Sing it loud and sing it strong;
Sing at Christmastime.

To the tune of "Twinkle, Twinkle, Little Star"

Sing a Christmas song with me;
It will make us hap-happy.
Christmas comes but once a year.
It brings happiness and cheer.
Sing a Christmas song with me;
It will make us hap-happy.

To the tune of "Oh Be Careful"

Oh come sing a Christmas song now with me.
Oh come sing a Christmas song now with me.
Oh come sing a Christmas song;
We will sing the whole month long.
Oh come sing a Christmas song now with me.

Recitation
S-I-N-G
Sing a Christmas song with me.

Recitation
When we sing a Christmas song,
It makes us happy all day long.

SS896

WHILE SHEPHERDS WATCHED THEIR FLOCKS BY NIGHT

WHILE SHEPHERDS WATCHED THEIR FLOCKS BY NIGHT is a display that encourages discussion about what people were doing the night of Jesus' birth. Use a dark-blue background, clothes of your choice, and a yellow or gold star. For a three-dimensional effect, use cotton for the sheep. A suggested color for the lettering is light blue.

SS896

WHILE SHEPHERDS WATCHED THEIR FLOCKS BY NIGHT

PURPOSE: To emphasize that life was going on normally the night Jesus was born. Stress that it was HE who made the night special.

SUGGESTED BIBLE VERSE: "And there were . . . shepherds . . . keeping watch over their flock by night." Luke 2:8

TABLE ACTIVITY: Make a shepherd and a lamb.

MATERIALS: Shepherd boy pattern from page 94, cotton, glue, movable eyes, pipe cleaners, dark-blue construction paper.

PROCEDURE: Prior to class, run off enough shepherds for each member of your class. Cut out. Have children glue the shepherd on the dark-blue paper and color him. Glue a pipe cleaner to the paper for the staff. Next, have them glue some cotton on the lamb. Glue the eyes on the Xs.

DISCUSSION: What do you think people were doing the night Jesus was born? Some people were working. The shepherds were at work taking care of their sheep. To them it was just like any other day. Work, work, work—that is, until the angel told them about Jesus! That made the day special!

CIRCLE TIME ACTIVITIES

Recitation

All the shepherds went to see,
Where the new Christ child could be.

A Story

And lo, there were shepherds sitting in their fields watching so the wolves wouldn't eat their sheep. Suddenly, a great light appeared. After they blinked a few times, they saw the light was an angel. They were so scared. "Don't be afraid, for I bring you terrific news! Tonight, Jesus, the Christ child, was born in Bethlehem." Quick as a wink other angels joined in to tell of Jesus' birth. When the angels had left, the shepherds hurried to Bethlehem so they could worship the Christ child.

To the tune of "Old MacDonald"

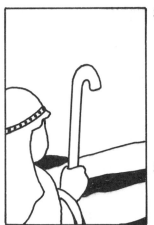

Shepherds watched their sheep that night,
Watched and watched and watched;
They were busy as could be,
Keeping safe their flocks.
Oh they watched, watched, watched,
And they watched, watched, watched.
Here they watched,
There they watched,
All they did was watch, watch;
Shepherds watched their sheep that night,
Of the Savior's birth.

Recitation

While shepherds watched their sheep one night,
A star shone down with glory bright.

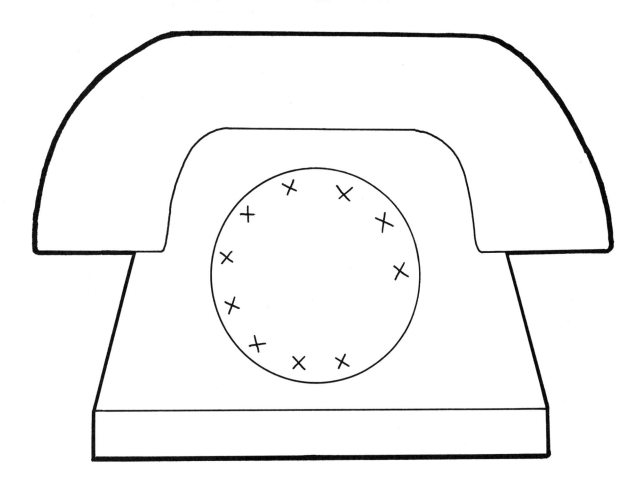

PRAYER CHANGES THINGS

Place on fold.

GOD'S LOVE
SETS US
FREE

SS896

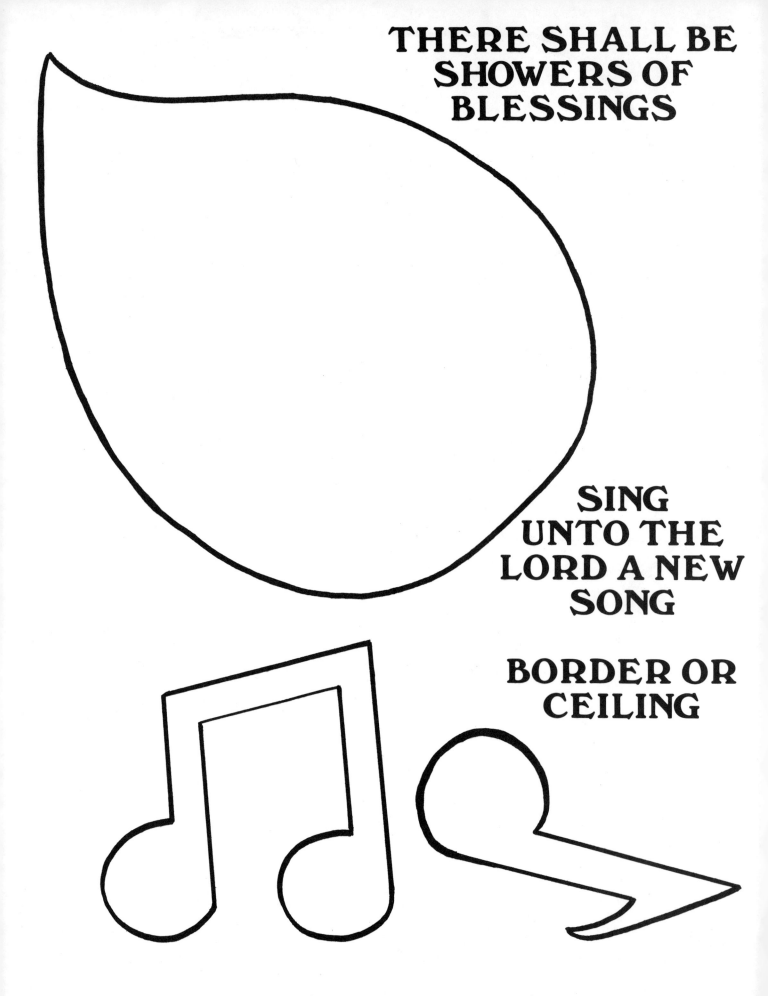

80

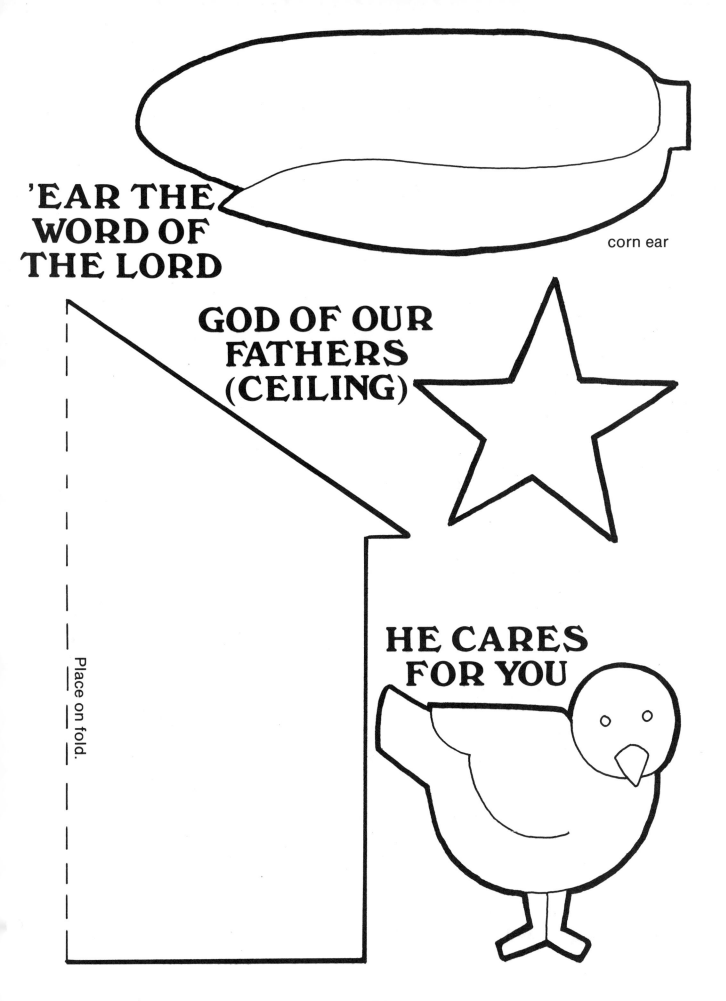

'EAR THE
WORD OF
THE LORD

corn ear

GOD OF OUR
FATHERS
(CEILING)

Place on fold.

HE CARES
FOR YOU

SS896

HOSANNA TO THE KING

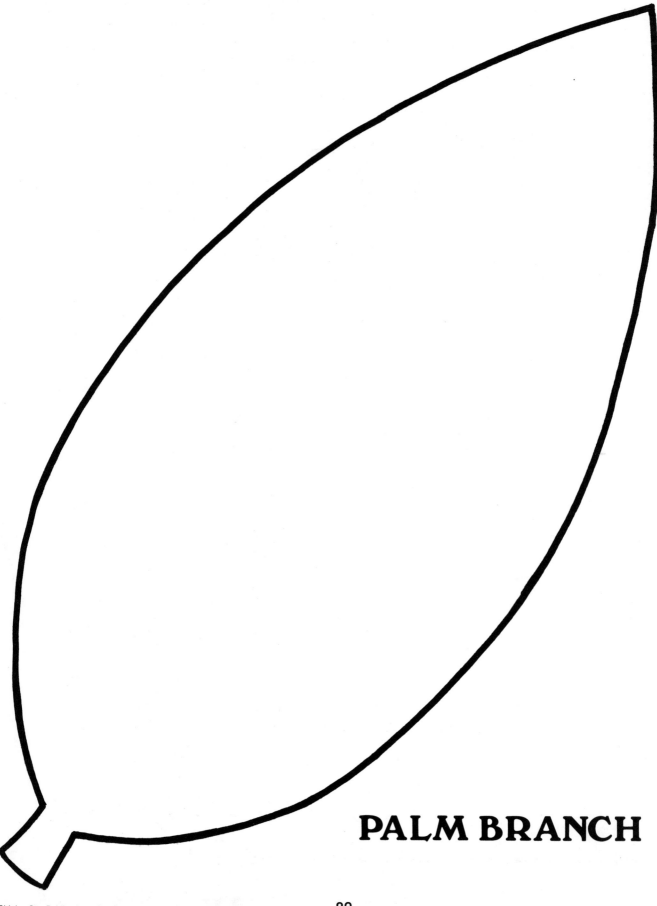

PALM BRANCH

SS896

HE AROSE!

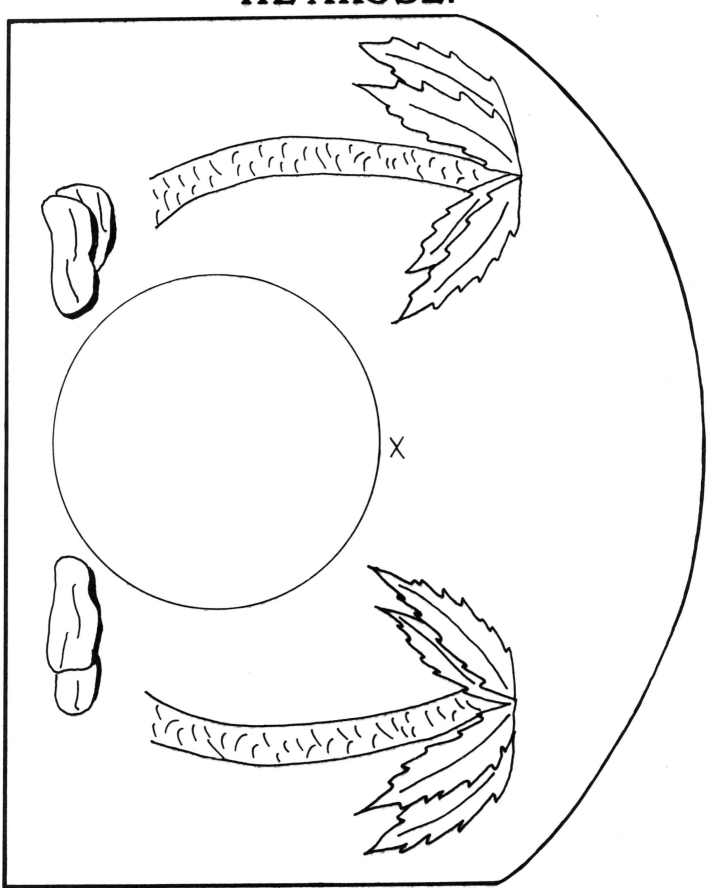

SS896

WORSHIP HIS MAJESTY

THIS IS THE DAY...

SS896

WORSHIP
HIS MAJESTY

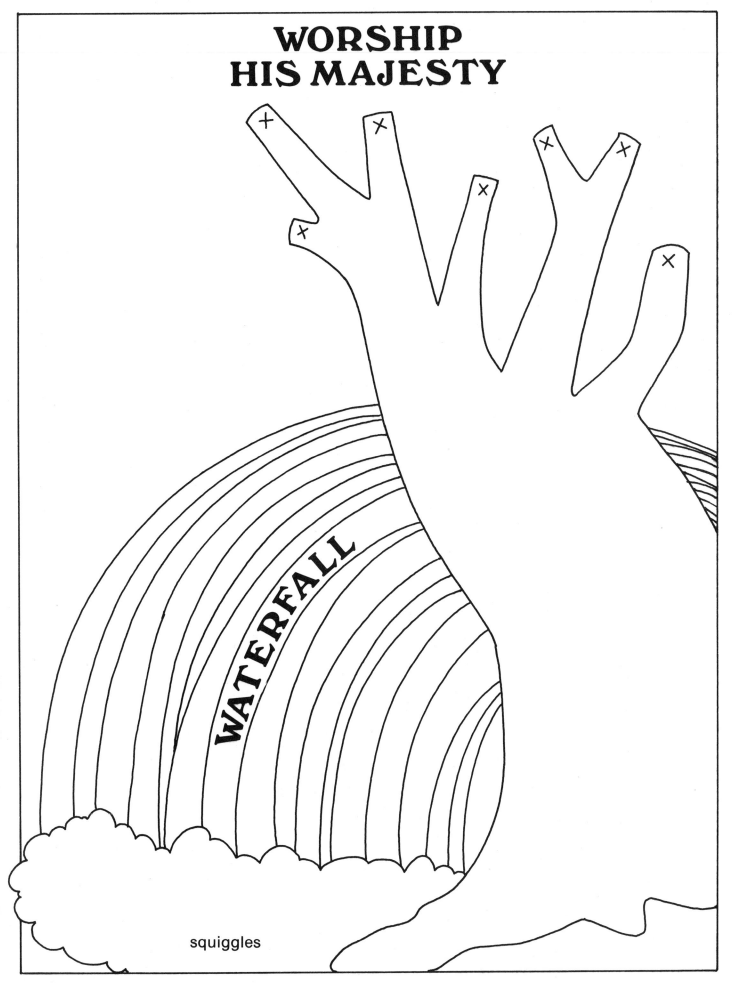

squiggles

SS896

I AM JESUS' LITTLE LAMB

CRAFT AND CEILING

JESUS LOVES EVEN ME

Place on fold.

WHO-O-O LOVES YOU

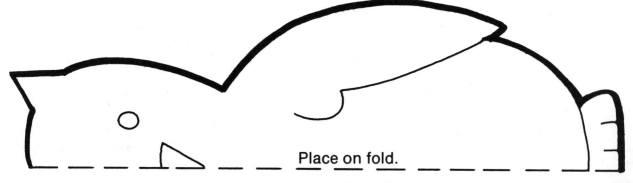

Place on fold.

SS896

FAITH OF
OUR FATHERS

ceiling

OUR COUNTRY!

SPRING

SUMMER

glue grass fringe here

TO EVERYTHING THERE IS A SEASON

FALL

glue
walnut
half
here

WINTER

SS896

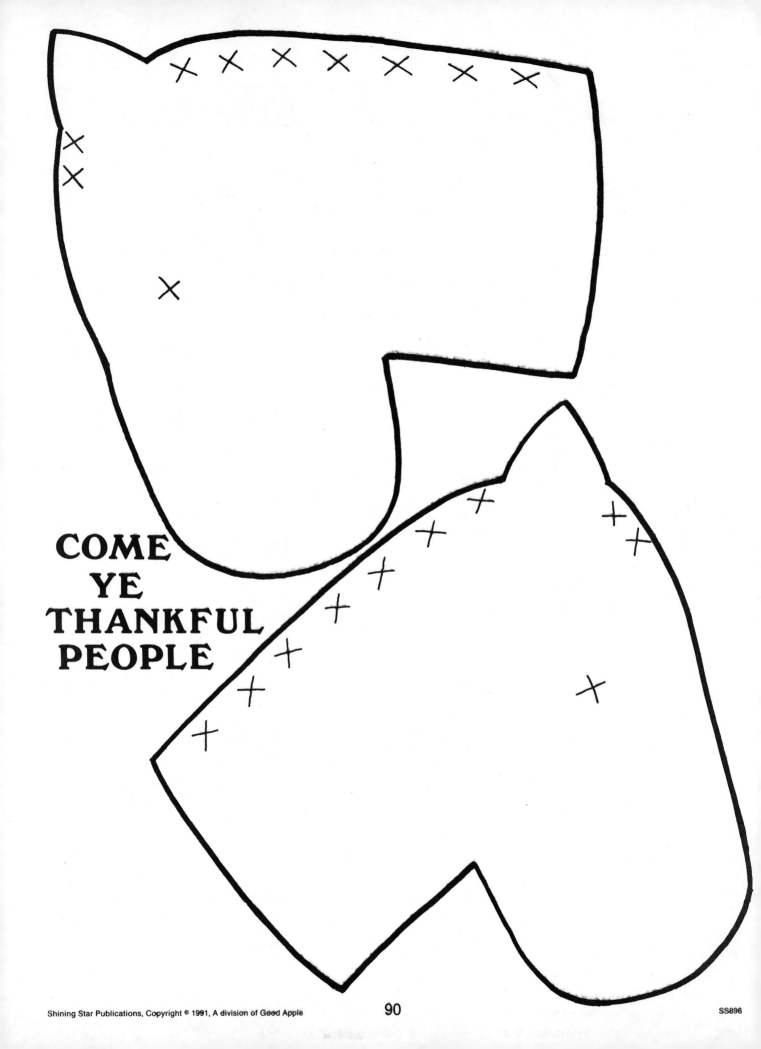

COME
YE
THANKFUL
PEOPLE

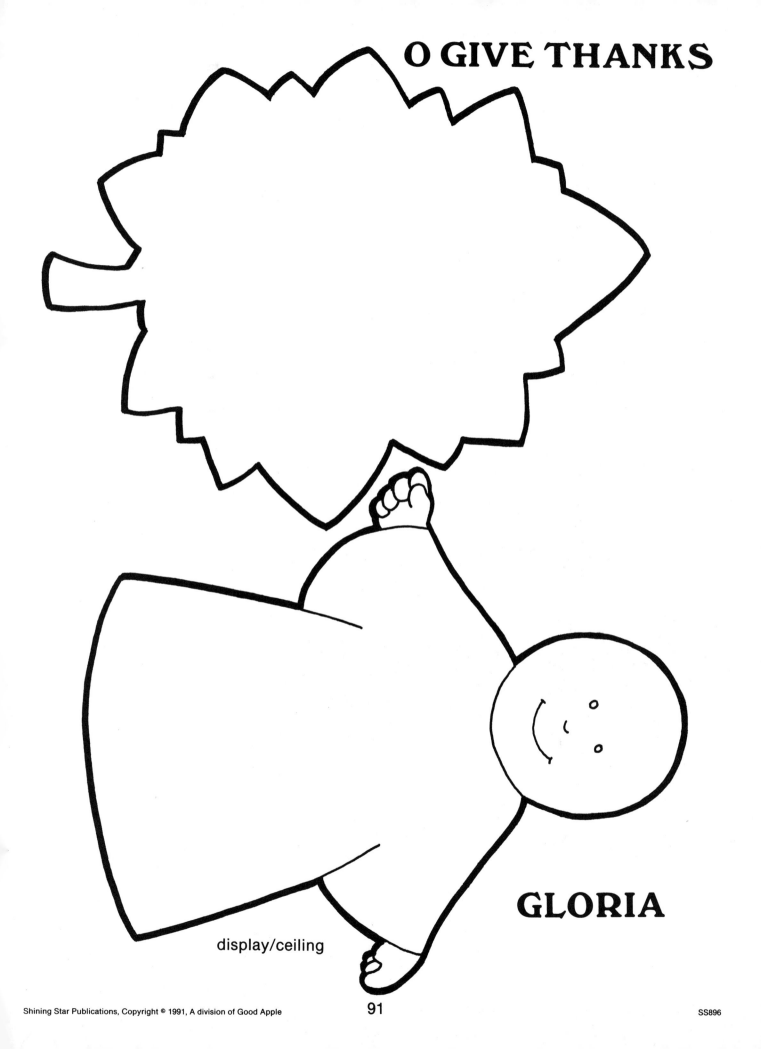

O GIVE THANKS

GLORIA

display/ceiling

91

O COME, LET US ADORE HIM

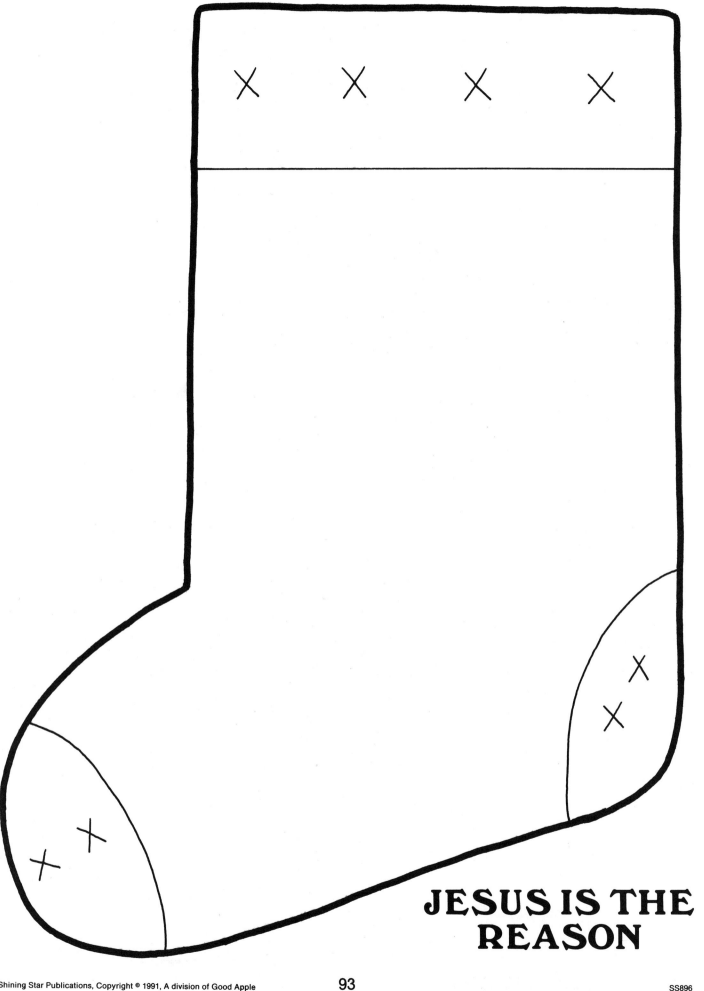

JESUS IS THE REASON

ceiling

WHILE
SHEPHERDS
WATCHED
THEIR
FLOCKS

SS896

ADDITIONAL CEILING AND BORDER PATTERNS

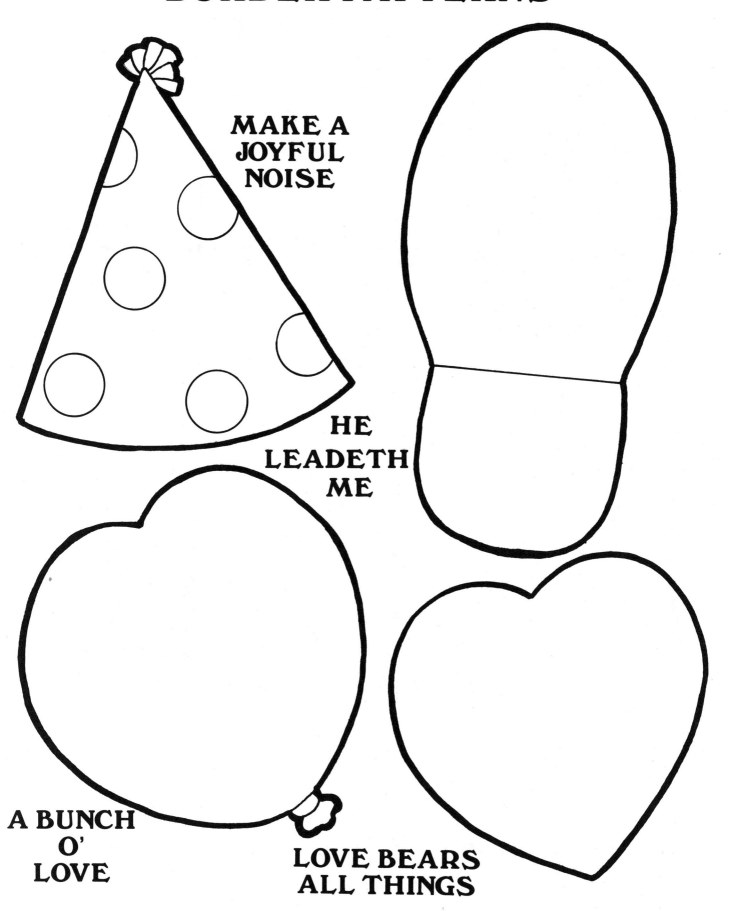

MAKE A
JOYFUL
NOISE

HE
LEADETH
ME

A BUNCH
O'
LOVE

LOVE BEARS
ALL THINGS

SS896

GOD'S LOVE SETS US FREE

PRAYER CHANGES THINGS

HOSANNA!

THERE SHALL BE SHOWERS OF BLESSINGS

96

SS896